Decorating
with
Plants
and
Flowers

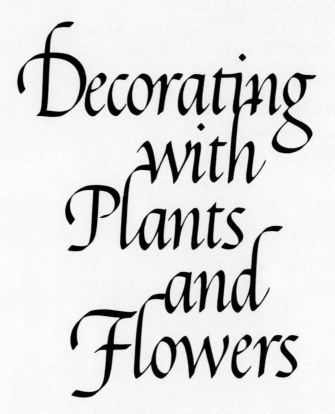

Decorating with Plants and Flowers

CHL CREATIVE HOME LIBRARY
In Association with Better Homes and Gardens
Meredith Corporation

CHL CREATIVE HOME LIBRARY

© 1972 by Meredith Corporation, Des Moines, Iowa
SBN 696-18900-3 Library of Congress Number 72-80747
All rights reserved
Printed in the United States of America

Library of Congress Cataloging in Publication Data
Main entry under title:

Decorating with plants and flowers.

1. House plants in interior decoration.
2. Flower arrangement.
SB449.D35   747'.9   72-80747
ISBN 0-696-18900-3

Contents

Introduction

Nature can live just as comfortably in a big-city high-rise apartment as it can in a home in the suburbs or a secluded country retreat. And the simplest and most satisfying way to bring nature into your home is by decorating it with growing plants and flowers.

As the concern for ecology has swept across the country, house plants and flower arrangements have taken on a new meaning. But much more important than this is the love people everywhere have for watching something alive and growing in their homes. This is true of people of all age groups—from youngsters who watch their minigardens or terrariums develop to grandparents who administer loving care to plants that may range from exotic tropical varieties to old-fashioned ferns and trailing ivies.

Architects and interior designers have long felt that in order to create a fine home setting with greenery and flowers it was necessary to incorporate built-in planters and ample natural or artificial light in their plans. But it has been only in recent years that homemakers themselves have fully realized the potential of plants and flowers as a valuable asset in home decorating—an asset that is equally as important as art objects and fine paintings.

Even though you have always loved plants and flowers for their natural beauty, you will find them still more rewarding if you consider them as a part of your decorating scheme. It may well be that a tiny nosegay of fresh flowers in a small crystal container provides just the right accent in your guest bedroom, while at the same time a tall treelike plant or a grouping of large plants commands attention as a major decorative feature. It's up to you to decide how and where you wish to use plants and flowers, but use them in every room of your home.

Follow the same basic decorating principles that you would use in choosing furnishings, fabrics, wall treatments, and floor coverings. Think in terms of color, texture, and scale when you choose your plants and flowers.

No longer is it necessary to be born with that mysterious power, a green thumb. The only quality you must have is a love for plants and flowers that makes you want to care for them. Just as with any other hobby, there are some people who have more of a natural instinct for indoor gardening than do others. If you are a beginner, choose plants that are easy to care for and inexpensive. And don't be too unhappy should your first efforts not be as rewarding as you had expected. A few minor setbacks will only add to the satisfaction you will feel when your first healthy plants add just the note you have always wanted in your home.

If you have areas in which it is virtually impossible to keep plants alive and healthy, consider the man-made plants and flowers—now called permanent plants and flowers because often they are so realistic—or arrangements of dried flowers and foliage.

We would like to give our thanks to Frederick H. Johnson and Yon Koski of Nature's Gallery, New York City, and Dick Volkamer, Hawkins Interior Plantings, Des Moines, Iowa, for their consultation on everything pertaining to plants in this book.

This sunny entryway from the terrace is an ideal spot for flowering plants and provides early color when the garden is not yet in bloom. The pink through red of the geraniums, hydrangeas, azaleas, and colorful caladium leaves echoes the terra-cotta brick while the green and white foliage leads the eye to the woods beyond.

CHAPTER 1

Coordinating Plants and Flowers with Your Decor

The use of house plants and flowers can add excitement to your decorating scheme. Though plants and flowers have natural beauty, you will enjoy them even more if you select varieties and colors that complement the style and colors of your furnishings, and if you place them just as thoughtfully as you would any other furniture or accessories.

Although almost all house plants and flowers seem at home in any surroundings, there are a few basic decorating principles that will show them at their best—color, scale, and balance. Use these as a guide when you choose your plants and flowers.

You may want color that strengthens the hues of your furnishings, or you may want color that contrasts sharply with a neutral background. In a large room you can use massed plants or a tall treelike plant. On the other hand, in a small room even a single plant or a few flowers carefully arranged can be the focal point.

You may choose a formal balance in the dining room—a floral arrangement centered on the table. On a mantelpiece you might place matching vases of flowers at either end. But in other areas you will probably select informal balance—a tall feathery plant balanced by a piece of furniture, or a ceramic vase filled with native grasses balanced by a piece of modern sculpture.

Whatever your decorating goals may be, there are plants and flowers to help achieve them, and often for a small investment.

Plants and flowers go with everything

Plants and flowers go with almost everything, but in order to achieve the best decorative effect, you should know some of the basic facts of colors and how to apply them.

Hue refers to the name of a particular color, such as red, yellow, blue, orange, green, or violet. Hues are pure undiluted colors.

Value has to do with a color's lightness or darkness. Colors that are nearer white in value are called tints. Colors that are closer to black in value are called shades.

Intensity, also called tone or chroma, is still another dimension of color. It refers to brightness or dullness. It is the degree of strength of a color. A pure color has a strong intensity. By adding gray to the same color, you lower its intensity. For example, green can be a clear intense color or, with the addition of gray, it can become a dull grayish green. The difference between these two greens is simply one of intensity.

When you add flowers, flowering plants, and other house plants to your color scheme you will find a wide choice of colors. Too often we think of flowers as hues, when in reality there are many subtle variations. And too often we think of plants as just green.

In nonflowering house plants there is an extraordinary range of colors, from the sooty black and emerald green of one prayer plant to the lacy white, pinks, reds, and greens of caladiums and the magentas, reds, yellows, starchy white, and greens of coleus; from the bronze blacks, bold golds, and reds of exotic crotons to the white, lettuce greens, and dark greens of dieffenbachias.

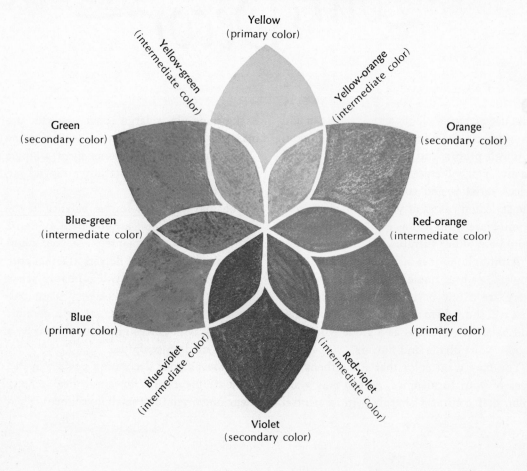

Yellow
(primary color)

Yellow-green
(intermediate color)

Yellow-orange
(intermediate color)

Green
(secondary color)

Orange
(secondary color)

Blue-green
(intermediate color)

Red-orange
(intermediate color)

Blue
(primary color)

Red
(primary color)

Blue-violet
(intermediate color)

Red-violet
(intermediate color)

Violet
(secondary color)

In the den-library above, the green and cream markings of the variegated rubber plant stand out against the red and black pinstripe fabric that covers the wall and the sofa bed. Bowls of red carnations and wax grapes and apples in a pair of scales complete the color picture.

In the living room below, a group of Queensland umbrella trees silhouetted against the sheer white draperies adds airiness and softness to a purely functional decor. The yellow daffodils in a modern crystal vase on the coffee table repeat the yellow and green of the color scheme.

Monochromatic color schemes

Monochromatic, or one-color, decorating schemes are built primarily around one color. But they utilize a range of tints, shades, and variations of that one hue. In order to keep this one-color theme from becoming monotonous, it is wise to add one or more neutrals—white, black, gray, or beige. These color schemes are easy to achieve and to live with.

It will help when planning a monochrom-atic color scheme to observe your natural surroundings—flowers, trees, water, earth, and the sky. You will immediately see that nothing in nature is all of a single color. The sky is a deeper blue overhead than it is near the horizon; trees and shrubbery appear in every imaginable shade of green. Instead of solid hues there are countless gradations and variations of each particular color.

Whatever color you choose, you can lighten or darken it, gray it or dilute it. For example, a monochromatic color scheme in blue might have light blue walls and draperies, a deeper shade of carpeting, and a still deeper shade for the sofa. Other pieces might be upholstered in a blue, black, and white plaid fabric with a tweedlike texture, or in a black and white houndstooth check. Add to this one-color scheme a mass of green plants, bowls of white and yellow flowers, bright wall hangings, and white lamps, and you will have a room that is anything but monotonous and dull.

The popular beige-to-brown earth tones also fall into this one-color category and are a natural backdrop for plants and flowers.

The room at the left features a monochromatic color scheme of gold with several touches of neutralizing black and white. The dark green leaves of the Madagascar dragon tree add contrast while the orange and yellow chrysanthemums on the lamp table complement the colors.

Red is such a bold and stimulating color that it takes only a very small amount of it in a monochromatic color scheme such as the one above. Team red with liberal doses of neutralizing black and white. Here the scheme is dramatized by adding a large bouquet of long-stemmed red roses.

Neutral color schemes

White, black, brown, and gray, with their many tints and shades, make up the family of neutrals. They are a popular choice for background colors and are particularly effective with unusual arrangements of plants.

White probably is the most widely used neutral. It provides an excellent background for any color scheme. For the multitude of homemakers who are renters, white is often a must. Many managers of rental property stick to white when decorating simply because it is the most neutral of all the neutrals and will not offend any prospective tenants. Whether or not you have white walls by choice, you can dramatize them with accents of green plants, bright-hued flowers, and flowering plants.

Black and white in combination have been a popular choice since the early days of the Roman Empire. You can achieve a dramatic

Neutral white and black are combined in the simple but sophisticated living room above. The furniture and accessories follow the same scheme to increase the emphasis on the Madagascar dragon tree, the Queensland umbrella trees, and the clear yellow in the art work on the walls.

In the living room at the right, a man-made reproduction of a pine serves as a piece of sculpture in bold relief against the warm beige tones of the carpeting, upholstery fabric, and draperies. Neutral black and white are used in large amounts and punctuated by small dashes of red.

color scheme with only these two neutrals by adding small doses of vivid color in the form of flowers, pillows, and lamps.

Brown, in its various shades and tints, can blend into either casual or formal rooms. Browns range from deep chocolate to very pale beige tints. Browns are especially compatible with such textures as brick, cork, and polished wood, and with textured wall coverings. If you choose dark chocolate brown for walls, use a large amount of white for contrast and to add light. If you have warm beige walls, continue the same neutral theme with carpet a shade deeper. Leafy green plants, flowering plants, and cut flowers with white, yellow, or bright orange blooms add a lively note to a neutral brown color scheme.

Gray ranges from charcoal to palest silver. It is basically a cool color, although there are some warm tints and shades. Gray in its lighter tones is a perfect background color for making a small room appear larger. Gray can support the brilliance of vivid colors in both furnishings and accents, so with it use lots of flowering plants and, in season, cut flowers with blooms of exciting colors.

White walls and white screens provide a neutral background for the yellow, green, and rust analagous color scheme above. The plants (clockwise from the left: cornstalk plant, dieffenbachia, lacy tree philodendron, piggyback plant, and Queensland umbrella tree) and the bowl of daisies add character to the simple but elegant room.

The sitting room on the right uses a red-violet and blue-violet analagous color scheme. The striking dried arrangement, the plant on the floor, and the table centerpiece of anemones are all scaled to the small dimensions of the room. The anemones and the apples on the coffee table provide touches of truer red.

Analogous color schemes

Analogous, or related, color schemes combine hues that are side by side on the color wheel. For example, yellow-green, yellow, and yellow-orange are an analogous color scheme because they have a common denominator—yellow. Look at the color wheel and you will see the possibilities in this combination. As each of the three colors has an enormous variety of shades and tints, you have great flexibility. This yellow-dominated color scheme provides an excellent opportunity to work plants and flowers into the decorating scheme. Green plants and flowering plants with yellow or orange blooms will strengthen the overall theme.

When you are planning an analogous color scheme, be sure to restrict your selections to not more than one-third of the color wheel.

Start with one color. Then look at your color wheel to see what the neighboring colors are. You can use these same three colors throughout your home simply by varying the value and intensity of each one. A different color can be the dominant hue in different rooms, with the two remaining colors in the secondary and accent roles. Use neutrals generously to vary the color scheme. No matter whether you are using subdued or bold colors, the coordination and repetition will provide a most harmonious result.

Another analogous color scheme, on the cool side of the color wheel, is blue, blue-green, and green. You can even use as many as five adjacent hues. Plants and flowers adapt well to this scheme too, and can be an integral part of the overall decorating plan.

Opposite or complementary color schemes

Opposite or complementary color schemes use colors that are opposite each other on the color wheel. Opposites can be red and green, orange and blue, yellow and violet, red-orange and blue-green, yellow-orange and blue-violet, or yellow-green and red-violet.

Because opposite colors are lively and vibrant, they must be apportioned carefully in a room. Using opposites means that there will be both a warm and a cool color in the room. It's best to let one of the colors dominate, and use variations of it in value and intensity according to the size of the room. A vivid color and its opposite can be subdued by reducing their values or by graying them. If the colors are not subdued, be sure to temper them with liberal amounts of neutrals.

Quiet colors for large areas such as walls and floors are soothing to live with. If you plan to use a red-orange and blue-green complementary color scheme, use a grayed tone of the blue-green for the walls and perhaps the floor covering too. Then use a brighter tone of the blue-green with neutral white or beige for draperies and upholstery fabrics, and use the red-orange in small doses—flowers, lamps, and accent pieces.

If your choice is a red and green complementary color scheme, use neutral white for the walls, green for the carpet and draperies, and a green and white fabric on upholstered pieces. Add large green plants, and introduce an arrangement of red roses, along with red accessories and accents.

A grouping of ferns in the corner and a bowl of yellow and white chrysanthemums on the glass tabletop add interest to the room at the left. The complementary color scheme, using the primary colors of blue and yellow with a small dash of red, originated from the painting on the wall and the porcelain plate on the table. The yellow and blue pillows repeat the basic color scheme while the oyster white of the sofa and the rug provides large blocks of neutralizing color.

The dining room above features a simple complementary color scheme of pink and green. The pink carnation centerpiece, as well as individual bouquets, napkins, and tapers, repeats the small amounts of pink in the floral wall covering, the checked fabric on the chair seats, and the decorative china. The wall covering and the sheer white fabric at the windows brighten up the traditional furniture, and the Boston ferns in the white wire plant stand add an airy touch.

Some cut flowers for home decorating

Flower Name	Approximate Length of Stem	Range of Colors	Keeping Qualities	Growing Season
African Daisy	Medium	White, many shades of yellow, salmon, orange	Good	Summer
Anemone	Medium	White, deep pink, scarlet, blue, lavender, mauve	Good	Late summer
Aster	Medium to long	White, pink shades, carmine, scarlet, red, lavender, blue shades, purple	Good to excellent	Fall
Calendula	Medium	Cream, yellow shades, apricot, deep orange	Good to excellent	Summer
Carnation	Long	White, pink to deep rose shades, salmon to orange shades; also, yellow, scarlet, red, deep red	Excellent	Summer
Chrysanthemum	Medium to long	White, many shades of pink and rose; also, bright red, brick red, bronze, salmon to orange, lavender, crimson	Excellent	Late summer and fall
Columbine	Medium	White, pink, blue, lavender, red, purple; most with white centers	Fair to good	Spring
Cosmos	Short to medium	White, light to deep pink, red, crimson, bi-color red with pink	Good	Summer
Cupid's Dart	Medium	Blue with dark center	Excellent (also to dry)	Summer
Daffodil (Narcissus)	Medium	White, yellow; also, white with trumpet yellow, gold, yellow-orange to deep orange; or yellow with deeper tone trumpet	Good to excellent	Spring
Dahlia	Short to medium	White, many shades of yellow, pink, orange, rose, lavender; also, purple, maroon, red	Good to excellent	Summer and fall
Daisy (Marguerite)	Medium to long	Yellow, white	Excellent	Summer
Delphinium	Long	White, blue shades, navy, lavender, purple, lilac pink to raspberry pink	Good to excellent	Early summer
Dianthus (Pinks)	Short to medium	White, many shades of pink; also, salmon, rose, scarlet, red, crimson, wine, variegated	Fair to good	Summer
Gaillardia	Medium	Many shades of yellow, orange, maroon, wine; also, yellow with red and red with yellow	Good to excellent	Summer
Gladiolus	Long	White, many shades of yellow, pink, orange; also, crimson, maroon, red, lavender, purple, violet	Excellent	Summer
Iris (Flag)	Long	White, many shades of yellow, pink, blue, lavender; also, purple, deep blue, maroon, bronze, brown; combinations of color	Good to excellent	Early summer
Iris (Japanese)	Long	White, pink, blue, purple	Good	Mid-summer
Iris (Siberian)	Long	White, blue shades, deep violet	Good	Late spring and early summer

	Stem length	Color	Keeping quality	Season
Larkspur	Long	White, shades of pink and blue, ruby red, mauve, scarlet	Good	Summer
Lilac	Medium to long	White, shades of lavender, pink, red; also, blue, blue-violet, red-violet	Fair to good	Spring
Marigold (short)	Short	Many shades of yellow, orange; also, rust red, tangerine, mahogany, red-edged yellow, yellow-blotched red	Good to excellent	Summer and fall
Marigold (tall)	Short to medium	Many shades of yellow, orange, deep orange	Good to excellent	Summer and fall
Narcissus (see *Daffodil*)				
Nasturtium	Short to medium	Many shades of yellow, orange; also, shades of scarlet and mahogany	Good to excellent	Summer
Pansy	Short	Many shades of yellow, blue, lavender; also, purple, bronze, mahogany, raspberry pink, violet; combinations of color	Good Excellent	Spring and summer
Peony	Long	White, many shades of pink and rose; cherry, crimson, salmon, ivory, garnet, maroon and deep reds	Excellent	Spring and early summer
Phlox	Long	White, many shades of pink; also, salmon, rose red, red, crimson, amethyst, blue	Fair	Late summer
Pinks (see *Dianthus*)				
Rose	Various	White, many shades of pink, yellow, orange; also, scarlet, red, crimson, salmon, blackish red	Excellent	All season
Shasta Daisy	Long	White, single with yellow center; also, all-white double	Good to excellent	Summer
Snapdragon	Long	White, many shades of pink, yellow, orange; also, cream, red, crimson, lavender	Good to excellent	Summer and fall
Stock	Medium	White, pink to rose shades, red, crimson, dark blue, purple	Good to excellent	Late spring and early summer
Strawflower	Various	Cream, shades of yellow and orange; also, salmon, rusty red, dark red	Excellent (also to dry)	Summer
Sweet William	Short to medium	White, shades of pink and rose, scarlet, red, crimson, wine red; also, variegated	Good	Summer
Tulip	Medium to long	White, many shades of pink, yellow, lavender, orange; also, violet, crimson, red, scarlet; red with yellow, yellow with red, cherry with white, etc.	Good to excellent	Spring
Zinnia	Medium	White, cream, many shades of yellow, pink, rose, lavender, orange; also, red, scarlet, salmon	Excellent	Summer and fall

CHAPTER 2

Room-by-Room with Plant and Flower Decoration

There are house plants and flowers that are suitable for every room in the home. At one time, a plant in the living room and a floral centerpiece on the dining-room table might have been considered sufficient. But in recent years professional decorators have rediscovered the charm and beauty that plants bring to interiors, so that today's home looks undressed without them.

The first consideration is to choose the appropriate plants and flowers. What would be suitable for a large living or family room might be overwhelming in an entrance hall. Plants that flourish where there is bright sunlight should not be placed in a windowless kitchen. The plants' colors should harmonize with the furnishings in the room.

Also consider the texture of the plants and flowers you want to use. Plants with large shiny leaves or flowers with glossy petals might blend perfectly with a contemporary decorating scheme, while lacy ferns or shaggy mum blooms might be the best choice for rooms with traditional furnishings.

Keep in mind the scale of the room or rooms you are decorating with plants and flowers. In a large room, you would use large plants or a grouping of smaller plants massed together. In a small room, such as a bathroom or a kitchen, you might choose to highlight a single small plant or floral arrangement.

On the following pages, you will find a room-by-room guide with suggestions for using plants and flowers in every room.

A cornstalk plant, a fern, and a bowl of yellow and white chrysanthemums highlight a Mediterranean living room that has furnishings of many textures in a variety of gold and brown tones.

In the living room above, with its blue and yellow color scheme sparked by large amounts of white, graceful trailing plants echo the room's tranquil spirit. Kangaroo vine and grape ivy are combined on the table. Pittsburgh ivy is on the mantel and one of the attractive bookcases displays both Pittsburgh and devil's ivy.

A tall cornstalk plant with its bladelike dark green leaves adds a dramatic note to the modern room at the right, and contrasts with the plump orange and yellow contemporary upholstery. The yellow and white spider chrysanthemums in the orange vase restate the color scheme.

Living rooms

To all who enter your living room, plants and flowers extend a friendly greeting and speak so eloquently of a serene home. Whether you are decorating a living room in a new home or apartment, redecorating an older one, or merely trying to add a little zest to your present decorating scheme, do remember to include plants and flowers as room accents. And no matter how small your living room is there is always a place for an attractive plant or arrangement of flowers.

If you are like most of us today, you probably spend more time, effort, and money decorating and furnishing your living room than any other single room in your home.

There are many reasons why people feel this desire to make their living rooms the highlight of their homes. One is that they enjoy a beautiful living room for their own use. Another is that it is the room where they most often entertain guests, and they want to be proud of it. Sometimes it is the only room in the home that visitors see. Still another reason might be that it is the most publicized and photographed room to appear in decorating books and magazines, and homemakers have access to ideas galore to adapt to their own living rooms.

As you pore over books and magazines for ideas that you can adapt to your own living room, you will notice that regardless of the style of the furnishings or what price range they fall in, invariably plants and flowers are included in the decorating scheme. You will notice too how carefully they have been selected to harmonize with the furnishings and how they are used as an integral part of the overall plan.

Look around your living room with a scrutinizing eye to see just which areas seem to lack something. It might be that you have a bare corner, and no piece of furniture seems to look exactly right there. In this case, why don't you place a house tree or large plant there? The size you choose will depend on the size of your living room—the larger the room is, the larger plant or house tree you can use. If there is still room to spare, group several smaller plants around the large one.

An unusual treatment which is bound to attract admiring glances and comments is an exceedingly tall container of glass or ceramic with long-stemmed foliage in a handsome composition. This shouldn't be a full, massive arrangement. Rather it is line, design, and simplicity that give it character and beauty. Try your hand at arranging tall stalks of spiked evergreen for a treelike slender effect. In the spring two or three long sprays of forsythia or a single branch of apple blossoms will make a striking arrangement. And leafy boughs from the country arranged in an old-fashioned umbrella stand can form a stunning effect. For a dramatic contemporary look arrange a few mums, bare branches, and vines in a tall cylindrical ceramic vase.

These are only a few suggestions, which might inspire you to dream up some of your own. Just remember to choose containers and flowers that suit your furnishings and the colors in your living room. And in the fall you can create the same types of arrangements with dried materials. These tall arrangements are ideal for a corner of the living room, one side of the fireplace, or in front of a large window.

The arrangement of yellow flowers and the feathery effect of the areca palm are completely in tune with the Oriental theme of the living room at the left, and the flowers echo the lamps and vases. The chairs and tables are finished in black lacquer, and the Japanese shoji screens at the window are covered with wall covering.

In the living room above, the warm color combination of rich hues of apricot, curry, and saffron is particularly good in a room that has stone walls. The handsome rusty fig in the corner with its russet tones and the gigantic bowl of yellow daisies complement the scheme.

When the floor space is limited in your living room, or there are small children and you wish to keep things out of their reach, use hanging baskets of tropical-looking ferns and trailing plants. Hang several of them in a bay window or from ceiling beams. You can even use an old birdcage; the larger it is, the more plants it will hold. If you don't have one tucked away in a storeroom, make a tour of the resale and thrift shops.

Living rooms in today's contemporary homes characteristically are simple in design, with expansive areas of glass that give an openness to interior spaces. This additional light affords good growing conditions for plants, and the background areas of natural materials—wood, brick, and stone primarily in neutral tones—need the warmth of plants and flowers to create a gracious home-like atmosphere.

The contemporary living room at the left, which overlooks a lake, has a miniature greenhouse of plants behind a clear plastic stand that supports the television set. Cactus plants share the windowsill with a telescope.

Rough-finished plaster walls, painted white and unadorned, provide a fine background for the Boston fern on the mantel and the tall Queensland umbrella tree. The dried arrangement in the yellow vase adds a note of subdued color.

If you have an older home, you may have a spot where you can install a built-in planter, or you can use a portable planter or a variety of plant and flower containers that will harmonize with your decor.

Not everyone may desire groups of large plants or masses of cut flowers in the living room. Some people can gain a great deal of pleasure from a single bloom in a small vase, or from a dish garden. Others like an easy-to-care-for terrarium filled with small green plants and moss.

But whether you buy large plants or small, do not choose them on their appearance alone or because you have the exactly right spots for them. First evaluate the light, temperature, and humidity in your living room and select only the plants that will thrive.

The large arrangement of yellow flowers in a crystal-clear container is the focal point in the living room at the left and reiterates the yellow and green decorating scheme. Hanging baskets of fern fill a bare corner and another fern on the table against the wall catches the lamplight.

Cooling off-white on the walls and floors in the living room below creates a pale shell for the yellow sofas. A spectacular basket of beautifully made silk flowers adds tremendous dash. Such a combination of colors could be duplicated with late spring flowers from the garden.

Halls and entryways

Halls and entryways are sometimes badly neglected or completely overlooked when it comes to home decorating. Actually the entrance hall should be at or near the top of your list of priorities. This is where people gain their first impression of your home and your family. And this impression often is the one that marks your home as inviting or uninviting, colorful or drab.

Very often there is not enough space in halls or foyers for many pieces of furniture. This is no handicap in good decorating, as there is no need for more than a small table or wall shelf and one or two chairs or a bench. A mirror is most important, and in fact almost necessary. It serves a real function as a kindness to your guests, who might wish to take a quick look when they come in from the outside, and it adds a needed dimension to the small space.

The next step is to add your own individual touch. One of the most effective tools with which you can create a distinctive atmosphere in halls and entryways is the use of plants and flowers. Plants, most particularly flowering plants, and fresh flowers always spell welcome to your guests and in the nicest way say, "We're glad you came."

When you have enough space, large plants or house trees can be placed on the floor in a bare corner. Or you might, in a long narrow space, place a row of several different kinds of plants along one wall. If you have a newer home or are building one, you may have a built-in planter in this area. Other good locations for large plants include the foot of an

This long dark passageway leading to a basement playroom was transformed into an inviting, theatrical entrance by a row of permanent plants in a mock planter, some copies of Toulouse-Lautrec posters, and some well-designed spot lighting that gives the plants a great air of reality.

open stairway or stairwell. Where floor space is limited, choose one tall slender plant rather than a round bushy one.

If your home is an older one, you may have a rather dark hall where the growing conditions for flowering plants are almost impossible. In that case take a tip from the many people who are handy with flowering plants. They simply rotate them. You can place some of your handsomest specimens in your front hall for a few days and then return them to their own place and bring out others. For festive occasions you might wish to bank them on a shelf or table. Be sure to light them well, not only for their health but also to bring out their true beauty. And flowering plants, like flower arrangements, almost double in size when they are placed directly against a mirror. As halls often have heavy traffic, do not put your most fragile blooms, such as fuchsias, there. Also see that your flower arrangements are not easily tippable.

It may seem extravagant unless you are giving a party to buy flowers for full-scale arrangements for your entrance hall. That is, unless your hall is really a foyer leading into your living room and therefore more or less

In the entry above, an antique bar chair is a conversation piece when the seat is used as a handy mail receptacle and a shelf is added below to hold a planter with some feather ferns. Leaves in a copper luster pitcher under the mirror add a parallel note of green.

In the entry at the right, the bouquet of yellow and orange flowers provides the one bit of contrast to the blue and white color scheme. A handsome bombé chest is flanked by a pair of matching chairs and above the chest is an antique mirror with matching wall sconces.

In the foyer at the left, a black and white color scheme is sparked with orange accessories and a cluster of orange flowers in a white bowl. A Madagascar dragon tree is dramatic against white walls. Both tree and flowers are reflected in the mirror, which adds to their impact.

a part of it. But you can, when a fine flower arrangement starts to collapse, retrieve the blooms that are still fresh, cut the stems back and place the flowers in a much smaller vase. The resultant little arrangement will add a note of living things and a touch of caring and feeling to a small hall or entryway.

If you have varying degrees of temperature in your entrance hall due to the frequent opening and closing of the front door and very little natural light, you may wish to use man-made or permanent plants and flowers.

No matter whether you use flowering plants, cut flowers, nonflowering plants, or permanent plants and flowers in your entrance hall, do see that the lighting is right—otherwise the drama will be lost. Splurge on spotlights and coved lights or whatever fits your needs so your plants and flowers will be presented at their best. Should you have large windows in your entryway, you might like to reverse the process and use hanging plants against the windows as a shimmering curtain wall lighted from within.

In the hall above, this fine plant has been given height by making a stand of an old Oriental jardiniere painted the same white as the walls. And it has been placed so it can be seen by anyone entering the door or coming down the stairs.

At the right, the large entry hall of an old home has been revitalized with carpet treatment and supergraphics in red and mauve. A dried arrangement of a single branch and a Queensland umbrella tree adds a further welcoming note.

Dining rooms

When your thoughts turn to a beautifully decorated dining room, you immediately envision the dining table centered with freshly cut flowers arranged in a handsome container. Unfortunately, most of us cannot afford this luxury daily unless we have garden flowers in bloom. So we are limited to the occasional dinner party when we buy cut flowers from the florist. However, there are numerous alternatives to the traditional table centerpiece that will create a welcome and congenial atmosphere in your dining room.

The average-sized dining room has just as many places to display foliage and flowering house plants as any other room of a home. There are window areas, buffets, serving tables, bare walls and corners, and even the dining table itself. Look around your own dining room to see just where you need something growing to complement your decor.

Because the furniture in the dining room is usually limited to a dining table and chairs, and one or more serving or storage pieces, the room probably lacks the large splashes of color provided by upholstered pieces in the living room or family room. So it is even more important to use house plants and flowers to add touches of color.

If your dining room has a lovely bay window with a southern exposure, this truly is an ideal location to display a group of plants and at the same time ensure healthy growing conditions. A bay window is also a good spot to display hanging baskets of ferns or trailing plants. Be sure to have window shades or curtains, shutters, or an outside awning installed because you need to carefully control the light during the daytime hours.

If you have a large empty corner that you wish to fill with something decorative, you might decide to place a tree-sized schefflera there. With adequate heat and light it will grow both tall and bushy. You might like to combine it with a kentia palm and several pots of fern. This is a good choice because their cultural needs are the same, and this

In the contemporary dining room at the left, the plants appear to be literally an extension of the outdoors seen through the sliding glass doors. The handsome Malay beauty on the buffet harmonizes with the house tree in one entryway and the fern on the freestanding fireplace.

The semiformal dining room above has a monochromatic color scheme of gold. To this the fake leopard fur cushions on the dining chairs add an important note of uncharacteristic color and mood, as do the fern and the stunning bamboo palm. And the unexpected combination of yellow roses and white daisies in the centerpiece is a light and whimsical touch.

combination provides contrasts in shape, leaf size, texture, and color.

Large-leaved philodendron, monstera, and devil's ivy are striking plants in dining rooms too. They can be trained on moss sticks, which give them height and the appearance of healthy, vigorous, mini-house trees. (See page 61 for the technique for growing plants on moss sticks.)

Flowering plants are also a welcome addition to dining rooms and will add sharp accents of color to your decorating scheme. Remember that some of the smaller, heavily blossomed, compact flowering plants can be massed together to make striking centerpieces.

There are some plants that bloom for brief periods only, but begonias and African violets are at the top of the list of those that bloom continuously. Geraniums, another all-time favorite, can be brought into two seasons of bloom in many regions.

Gloxinias, clivias, and amaryllises are all blooming favorites that are truly seasonal plants and are meant to be enjoyed even though their blooming period is brief. Also, there are the bulb plants—hyacinths, daffodils, and tulips—which will lift your spirits during the late winter-early spring months because you can grow them indoors long before they bloom in your garden.

The texture of the spider aralia in front of the Japanese screen adds softness to the contemporary dining room at the left, as does the floral arrangement in the black ceramic vase. The yellow and green accent the black and white wall covering and the molded white plastic furniture.

In the dining room below, pots of flowering plants instead of flowers are used for an unusual centerpiece. The blossoms pick up the shade of red in the tableware, the hanging light fixture, and the pattern in the drapery fabric.

Family rooms

Family rooms may be geared for activities and conversation, but this doesn't mean that the decor is any less important than it is in the rest of the house. Whether only members of the family make use of the room or whether it is also used for entertaining guests, you will want it to be as colorful and pleasant as you can make it.

It wasn't too many years ago that the family room, more commonly called the recreation ("rec") room, was a remodeled area in the basement. Usually the furniture was a collection of discarded items from the rest of the house, and the only natural light was the little gleaned from high basement windows. Today the family room has moved to the main floor of the house because it has been planned that way, and so there is often natural light for growing plants. And in newer homes the family room is sometimes larger than the living room. In many homes it is the hub of family activity, and with its vital role in today's families, its decoration is important.

Probably the two most popular styles of decorating for family rooms are country and contemporary. Even though each portrays a distinctly different mood, the reason for their wide acceptance is that both are attractive

A magnificent weeping fig, almost ceiling high, sets the key for the light and airy room on the left belonging to a family of music lovers. Smaller plants on the end table and by the piano repeat the green-against-white motif.

The warm tones of the wood and the brick floor in the family room above are accentuated by the Christmas kalanchoe on the counter, the dried bittersweet on the top shelf, and the copper utensils. A miracle plant stands by the window.

and durable and can withstand more than the normal amount of daily use.

Regardless of the decorating style you choose for your family room, you will want to incorporate some plants and flowers into the total scheme. If the room is used for many activities, display your plants and flowers where they will add decorative interest but at the same time will not interfere with games, hobbies, or social functions.

In the plant grouping in the family room above, feather ferns in clay pots, all in a row on the top bookshelf, balance the large cornstalk plant in the corner. The geometric wall covering inspires the decorating scheme—choice of colors, patterns, furniture, and accessories.

With imagination you can turn a storage wall into an ever-changing background of plants, dried arrangements, statuary, and entertainment components. The free-standing wall in the family room at the right is a tension pole unit system placed around the electric organ.

If gardening is your hobby, the family room may be the ideal place for you to install an indoor garden and carry on your hobby all year. You could design and build an indoor garden with built-in planters, shelving, and a lighting arrangement. Should you not have a large enough corner for a garden, you could build it up one wall. Here is the chance to use your landscaping talents and produce a show-piece for the family. You might wish to specialize in exotic tropicals which are always so impressive. Or you might want to add some unusual rocks in a Japanese-inspired effect. And if you have some interesting shells or pieces of driftwood collected on vacation trips, you might combine them with plants—always an effective way to display their beauty. This is also true of fine, small sculptures.

Kitchens

Today's kitchens are planned primarily for function and convenience. It's up to you to add the personal and decorative touches that will make your kitchen a pleasant room in which to plan and prepare meals.

With this in mind, what better device can you use than living green or flowering plants and herbs? It doesn't matter whether you have ample room for a variety of plants or such limited space that you can display only a few; something live will add immeasurably to your kitchen.

Strips of fluorescent lights installed below the wall storage units in the remodeled kitchen above make the shelf into a space-saving place for herbs and decorative plants. Sprengeri fern, Christmas cactus, and staghorn fern mingle with sprouted shallots and culinary herbs.

In the kitchen at the right, the window wall and generous counter space make a perfect spot for a collection of plants that will bloom all year, adding warmth to the cold, functional equipment and transforming a bleak winter view.

Geraniums, African violets, and tuberous begonias are all flowering plants that are favorites for kitchen window sills, as they add such a warm and cheery note. For those dreary days at the end of the winter you might wish to add an advance touch of spring to your kitchen by forcing pots of bulbs—tulips, hyacinths, and daffodils.

To put a little spice in your kitchen, why not raise some herbs? They are not only attractive but also provide wonderfully fresh flavorings for your cooking. Dill, bay, basil, chives, rosemary, mint, sage, and thyme are all herbs that can be grown in the kitchen. If you have had the disheartening experience of buying potted herbs or prepackaged herb kits by mail and having them disintegrate into a mess of brown tumbleweed in a short time, the fault may lie in the pot. Usually these plants are sold in two-and-a-half-inch mini-pots or frail plastic trays because they are lightweight and easy to ship. These pots are not large enough for healthy plant growth, and the plants should be transferred to larger pots almost immediately. It is best to place your pots of herbs in a sunny window or hang them in brackets on the inside of the casement where they can take advantage of the light. And use your herbs generously. Clipping and pinching back will improve their appearance by keeping them from getting leggy, and will help them produce.

If you have one of those dream kitchens with expansive windows that let in lots of natural light, you can choose from a multitude of plants and have the pleasure of working in what is almost an indoor garden. In a kitchen with much less light, or a windowless apartment kitchen, you can still grow some plants by artificial light.

Bedrooms

Once there was an old wives' tale that plants in a bedroom used up the "good" air and were bad for the health. Now, of course, we know that plants, unlike people and animals, breathe carbon dioxide and give off oxygen. Or as some of today's ecologists say, every time we plant a blade of grass we are doing the world a good turn.

Unfortunately the old belief has left echoes of which we are quite unconscious. And without considering the why, many of us somehow do not think of putting plants and flowers in our bedrooms. There are so many reasons why we should.

What else but plants and flowers could extend such a cheery greeting when you first open your eyes in the morning and contemplate the busy schedule ahead of you? Too, there is the odor, barely definable, of growing plants—an air-cleansing odor. Perhaps it is all that oxygen they are giving out. Then there is the subtle fragrance of many of the cut flowers. Certainly when you have house guests you try, if it is at all feasible and flowers are in season, to have at least a little nosegay on the bedside table and perhaps another on the dressing table to delight the eyes of your guests when they wake up. Surely you should do as much for yourself.

There's another very good reason, quite apart from our personal pleasure, why we should have plants and flowers in our bed-

rooms. We have become accustomed to using our living space in far more flexible ways, and we no longer think in the old categories of bedroom, living room, dining room, and kitchen. Instead, we ask ourselves how we live and how we use the various rooms.

Your bedroom may be your place of retreat, where you and your husband read, watch your own TV, or catch up on letters and work. If it is your private living room and study as well as your bedroom, you might plan the decor as a bed-sitting room. In doing so, remember that nothing will give more of a sitting-room quality than handsome plants. Use them along with books and pictures just as you would in a living room, though in a more informal manner as befits a sitting room. With a room of such dimensions that you can divide the sleeping and the study-living areas, you might consider how plants can emphasize the line of demarcation by being arranged as a partial "wall" or "curtain."

On the other hand, if you use other rooms for your work and hobbies, and your bedroom is small and has ample closet and dressing-room space, your furniture needs are simple. Then, instead of adding character and

In the combination bed-sitting room at the right, an armoire and a tall, handsome permanent (manmade) bamboo serve as room dividers, mark the entryway between the sleeping area and the sitting area, and provide a sharp contrast with the vivid red and white color scheme.

In the bedroom at the left, with its vibrant red monochromatic color scheme, strategically placed plants provide a change of pace. Several different plants, including green and white striped dracaena, are massed in the corner for the focal effect. Boston ferns on the dresser and a bedside plant repeat the green.

spirit with color and fabrics, you could transform your bedroom into a garden bower with sunlight flooding through hanging plants at the windows and onto banks of plants on stands and on the floor.

Long in the past the bedroom was solely the wife's room. Unfortunately, in the reaction against an overly feminine decor a rather static and neuter decorating scheme took its place. The result was a room that was neither his nor hers, a room that made no statement at all about the people to whom it belonged. If you are in rebellion against such a bedroom, you might think of what colors you and your husband both enjoy and whether you have a joint collection you are particularly fond of and would like to make into a decorating point. Then add your individual preferences. He may choose a Winslow Homer print. You may want one pink-apricot wall. No matter, put it all together. A generous quantity of plants will join the disparate elements and provide a dominant theme. As every landscape architect knows, greenery is a miracle worker at creating harmony.

And while you are considering your own bedroom, you might think of your children's. Just as the young enjoy small animals, they love to see things grow. Plants in their bedrooms can be a learning as well as an enjoying experience. With the very young it is best to concentrate on the fast-growing plants which will startle and delight them and on

In the young girl's bedroom above, the green and white plaid curtains and bedspreads, the lightly scaled black and brass bed, and a freshly painted chest make the most of a small room. The unusual planter holds an appropriate arrangement of green fern and creamy white snapdragons.

In the small bedroom at the left, the mellow apricot walls and the stripped-down wooden trunk are restful alongside the gleaming brass bed. The large arrangement of leaves in the tub on the floor adds just the right touch and, unlike flowers, is long lasting and does not require care.

the highly neglectable plants. While it is good for them to learn to water and care for plants, there will be times those plants go thirsty. The succulents with their ability to withstand drought are a natural for this. There are the many varieties of sedums, and such interesting shapes as the echeverias, with their tall, yellow-topped stalks, and hens-and-chickens. While cactus plants fascinate the young and need little watering, there are those spines; it is best to put them off until considerably after kindergarten age. Another thing that delights children is growing plants from seeds. Avocado pits can be rooted in water and are fairly fast growers. Grapefruit, orange, and lemon seeds make endearing seedlings. And perhaps by the time your child goes off to college you will have a handsome citrus tree.

In the room above, which serves as sitting room as well as bedroom, the "living room" ambience has been firmly established with the grayed blue walls, the magnificent glossy-leaved house tree, and the unusual love seat made from a child's brass bed. The colors in the art work and the pillows add further to the nonbedroomy air.

Bathrooms

No longer is the bathroom merely a room in which to shower, bathe, or wash your hair. Not too many years ago, bathrooms in this country were cold and purely functional. Gradually they have given way to convenient, but fairly glamorous, settings. Now in the bathroom, as in every other room of the home, comfort is a requisite—not just the comfort of the right fixtures, but the comfort of having a happy color scheme, adequate storage area, good lighting, a practical floor plan, and carefully chosen accessories.

Even though your bathroom fixtures may have no particularly distinctive design, you can establish a decorating style—country, traditional, contemporary, or eclectic—with the selection of wall and floor coverings, shower curtain, linens, and decorative accessories.

And there are many ways in which by using light colors, dark colors, warm colors or cool colors you can change the proportions and ambience of your bathroom. If it has too little natural light, try to stay with the light, warm colors and use the darker and cool colors as occasional accents.

When you select accessories from towels and shower curtain to pictures, soap dishes, jars, and mirror frames, you can mix or match colors, patterns, and stripes. By combining different ones at different times you can have a complete change of pace.

The humidity which is present in most bathrooms makes them an ideal place for many kinds of plants. Philodendron, fittonia, Chinese evergreen, and grape ivy are among those that will do well with little care in such an environment if there is some natural light.

If your bathroom is large enough you can arrange a grouping of plants in containers on the floor in a garden-like setting. If your floor space is limited you can display plants on the

The powder room at the left is small and windowless, but the predominantly red wall covering and the red washbowl give it an inviting look. The frankly and playfully artificial flowers repeat the red as well as the blue. And the well-composed arrangement of permanent plants under the mirror adds a softening touch.

Don't be discouraged if you have a vintage bathroom of the early thirties like the one on the right and you aren't ready to undergo major remodeling of tile work and plumbing fixtures. The two tremendous baskets of ferns placed together in a cascade effect with the light showing through add warmth to the somber blue, detract from the exposed pipes, and lower the high ceiling. The white and black wall covering and the off-white floor covering add lightness.

vanity, on shelves, or in hanging baskets.

Many bathrooms—especially in new apartments—have no windows. If the bathroom is spacious, this would be a good room to get started growing a few plants under fluorescent light—installed on a shelf or table. The windowless bathroom is also an ideal place for small permanent plants—for example, on either side of the mirrored cabinet on small shelves, or on a corner of the bathtub.

Whenever possible place a few cut flowers on your bathroom vanity or window sill. If you have your own garden you can use them lavishly and replace them often during the blooming season. If you have to buy your cut flowers you can still achieve a striking effect with only a few flowers and some green leaves. Or you may choose to purchase a few very fine permanent flowers which will complement your color scheme.

The owners of the bathroom on the left enjoy both traditional and contemporary decor. The fake stained-glass window, dark paneling, and oval mirrors are reminiscent of bygone eras while the light fixture and lavender counter spell today. The ever-popular Norfolk pine in the corner somehow ties the pleasing mixtures together.

The understated elegance of the bathroom below depends on the ivory, white, and black color scheme and the restrained use of classic patterns. There are two welcome softening touches —a luxurious fur rug and the arrangement of pale yellow flowers and baby's breath.

CHAPTER 3

House Trees and Other Striking Greenery

It isn't always necessary to travel to faraway places to find a junglelike atmosphere. You can create your own minijungle with a tall treelike plant, other large plants, and hanging baskets or containers of trailing plants in your living room or family room.

If you have a large room that you wish to bring alive by adding growing things, why not mass several large plants in a corner location? You can start with a tall, regal palm and group several ferns and one of the scheffleras or umbrella trees around it. These are all compatible in their growing needs—light, heat, and humidity—and still there are contrasts in their forms and leaves.

In front of a large window you might add an arrangement of hanging containers and pots of plants that would make a curtain of greenery and give a feeling of height.

Consider the size of your room, the colors, and the style of your furnishings. Do you want to spotlight a single large bushy plant or tall narrow one, or do you prefer a grouping of several sizes and varieties? Do you like large, boldly formed leaves or graceful, delicately shaped leaves? Will leaves with a shiny, waxlike appearance provide the accent you desire, or is your preference for leaves with a soft, velvety finish? Weigh all these features carefully, as well as the all-important requirements for growth—whether the plants that fit your decorative scheme will thrive under the light, temperature, and humidity conditions in your home. Different species suit different environments, and you might like to get professional advice as to just which are best for the growing conditions in your home.

In this formal living room, plants are used with such dramatic flair that they take on as much importance as the furniture. The imposing grouping on the left was chosen for contrasting textures —kentia palm, weeping fig, and Norfolk pine. And the bird's-nest fern in the urn underlines the Regency flavor of the decor.

53

House trees

A tall, impressive house tree may require a sizable dollar investment, but it can be as dominant a force as an unusually handsome piece of furniture or striking sculpture.

Some of the more common varieties of plants that stretch up to the ceiling are palms, scheffleras, rubber plants, dracaena fragans (cornstalk plants), dracaena draco (dragon trees), *Ficus cyathistipula* (thin fig), and some camellia and citrus trees. Choose a container that is scaled to the size of the tree, and is in a color and design that contribute to the overall decorating scheme of the room.

Once you decide on such a plant, study its placement as thoughtfully as you would that of any large piece of furniture, since it will require a special setting. Usually the best place is a sunny corner or in front of a window wall. Try to put it where it can be seen from any part of the room, so it can assume its place as an important part of the decor. And do keep it away from normal traffic.

The living room at the left uses a zebra-patterned sofa, one large painting, and a whopping big cornstalk plant to play up white walls. Old-fashioned high-ceilinged rooms such as this are a natural foil for large-sized house trees.

In the living room below, the tall jagged shape of the Madagascar dragon tree provides the essential element in a decorating scheme that otherwise is on the verge of being too low keyed, too restrained, and without a feeling of height. The dried arrangement repeats the same line.

The dare-to-be-different black-burlap-covered walls above make a fine background for prints and decorative brass. And they show off the green of the man-made punting-pole bamboo behind the sofa, which adds a seemingly natural note where no real plant could grow.

The full umbrella tree behind the desk at the right helps divide the dining ell from the rest of the living room and contributes the needed green of growing things to the subtle but somewhat austere color scheme of varying shades of gun-metal and black and white glen plaid.

Large plants

Because they are living things, plants are sometimes more personal than many decorative accessories. And there is hardly a better or more satisfying way to decorate a bleak corner or a large expanse of bare wall than with large plants. Think in terms of scale and the style of your furnishings, and choose plants large enough to erase the empty look —but not too many or too large, as there should be no overcrowded feeling.

Some of the varieties of large plants are split-leaf philodendron, fiddleleaf fig, dieffenbachia, podocarpus, monstera, nephthytis, palm, jade plant, and Norfolk pine. In addition, there are even some varieties of cactus that could fall into the category of large plants. Also, many vining plants which are trained on moss sticks will grow tall and bushy enough to be classified as large plants. You can expect these large plants to grow from two to six-feet tall. (See pages 122-125 for growing requirements.)

Look around your home, and you will find many places to use large plants. A bay window is a natural spot for a grouping of several sizes and varieties of plants. A stairwell is an ideal location for large plants; an expansive window wall is another; an empty corner is still another. If you have a low chest or bench, why not put a fiddleleaf fig or schefflera plant about two or three feet high on it? Be sure to give it a handsome container.

It could be that what you consider the ideal location for your large plants from a decorative standpoint is sadly lacking in natural daylight. If this is the case—and it's a common one—don't relinquish your plans. Instead, consider the possibility of supplementing the natural light by installing additional fixtures for artificial light. Ceiling spots or recessed lighting directed toward the plant or plants will often solve your growing problem and will provide additional drama as well.

Mirrors in the lower panels of one wall in this living room add dimension to the wide-leaf rubber plant. And the plant's solid, simple form reflects the character of the room, with its Oriental rug and classic modern furniture.

Moss sticks

Plants with vining tendencies are a popular choice for decorating, as they can be trained on moss sticks. If you are budget minded, you can purchase inexpensive young vining plants and raise them to the desired height over a period of time. Also, they are easy to grow.

A moss stick is simply a column of hard-ware cloth or wire netting stuffed with sphagnum moss and set in a deep pot filled with earth. A plant growing on a moss stick should be watered through the column as well as the earth in the pot. This will provide moist growing conditions for the aerial roots the plant will produce as it climbs the stick. Watering in this manner is very important for maintaining a lush and healthy growth.

Devil's ivy grows well on a moss stick, although it grows more slowly than common philoden-dron. It needs stronger light than monstera, if you wish to keep the white splashes in the leaves, and it gives you a slender pillar of green.

Aristocratic monsteras such as this Mexican bread-fruit adapt well to home growing conditions. They tolerate any exposure except direct sunlight. They grow best in a moist atmosphere, which the stick provides if it is properly watered.

Groups of plants

A group of plants can be a major element in your decorating scheme. But when grouping them, you must arrange them as carefully as you would a collection of prints or porcelain figurines. And more than that, the plants themselves should be in keeping with the spirit of your decor.

A starkly modern interior begs for plants of bold outline. A turn-of-the-century scheme demands a seemingly fussier though equally well arranged effect that gives a feeling of artful clutter and nostalgia. A formal eighteenth-century dining room requires large-scale, dignified plants, while early American furniture is happier with tidy, unpretentious ones that reflect the quality of the furniture.

The windows of the Edwardian room at the left are uncurtained. Instead, an artfully arranged group of plants framing the windows—on stands and hanging—gives them color and a feeling of pattern. The reds, greens, and yellows of the coleus are reminiscent of the period.

The plants above were chosen carefully for the hall and stairway. From left to right, they are: Indian laurel, neanthe bella, flowering inch plant, and calamondin orange. The composition and clean bold lines of the group complement both the modern architecture of the house and the period furniture used here.

When you group your plants, aim for variety in size, leaf texture, form, and color. Place the taller ones toward the back, of course, and the shorter ones forward.

Another consideration is to group varieties of plants together that have similar light and humidity requirements. Basically, these fall into three categories: low light and average humidity; medium to bright light and average humidity; medium to bright light and high humidity. For example, jade tree, Norfolk pine, and podocarpus can be combined in one group because they have similar light and humidity requirements. (See pages 124-125 for the growing requirements for flowering plants, pages 122-123 for requirements for nonflowering plants.)

Whether you group plants on the floor or on a wide window sill or shelf, guard against water damage. You can use shallow plant trays of metal or plastic lined with an inch or so of pebbles. Set the pots on top, and the excess water will drain into the pebbles. Or use plastic utility mats with deep rims and raised grid surfaces, or set the plants on pieces of clear plastic or cork.

The Madagascar dragon tree, the red emerald philodendron, and the sweeping arc of the contemporary lamp provide a dramatic background for the around-the-corner seating pieces in the living room at the left. Yellow, red, and blue accents reinforce the dark green of the plants.

One wall of the family room above has been made into a subtropical garden. Clockwise from left to right: heartleaf philodendron, Florida philodendron, towering thin fig, and lady palm and fern palm against a background of podocarpus. All are lit by a skylight overhead.

The tiny home office above of a big-city apartment could seem claustrophobic. But plants on the floor, desk, and shelves give the illusion of wide open space so cherished by urbanites. Hanging baskets of plants (mostly ivy) take the place of curtains and let in more light.

Two splendid baskets of Boston fern are used to dress the bay windows of the turn-of-the-century home at the right. The furnishings are a comfortable mix of modern pieces combined with mellow old pieces from many periods. Red roses on the burl table pick up the red and the green.

Hanging plants

Hanging plants have become enormously popular lately, and with good reason. They don't take up floor space, and a hanging plant can be as artful as a mobile.

Hanging arrangements can even take the place of curtains where complete privacy isn't necessary. The hanging plants are compatible with any style of furnishings—traditional, contemporary, country, or eclectic.

Tropical-looking and feathery-looking ferns, English ivy and kangaroo vine, old-fashioned philodendrons, and ivy geraniums are plants that will grow well in hanging baskets. All of these will thrive in bright light and will not suffer from the cooler temperatures found near large windows in wintertime —as long as the low temperature near the windows is not less than 65 degrees.

Wet soil is heavy, so the ceiling must be in excellent condition before a plant can be hung from it. A better way is to hang plants from a strong rod near the top of a window.

CHAPTER 4

Flowers and Small Plants as Room Accents

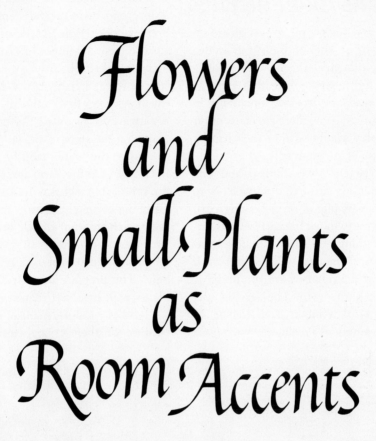

Flowers and small plants, both the nonflowering and the flowering varieties, can be effective accents. Even though you choose them for their beauty, be sure that they are also a part of the total decorating scheme.

Flowers and plants with blooms of vivid colors can provide a sharp accent in a room decorated primarily in neutral tones. For example, in a room where brown and beige tones predominate, bright yellow tulip plants in the spring and yellow chrysanthemums in the fall would be ideal blooming plants. And in these same surroundings such cut flowers as orange and yellow zinnias, yellow daisies,

or daffodils would add just the right amount of bright accent. For a room whose decorating scheme stems from a vibrant hue such as red, blue, or yellow, choose plants and flowers with cool, creamy white blossoms that inject a note of serenity into the decor.

Nonflowering plants, too, can be important accents. You can group several small varieties together in a display, or you can spotlight one small, exquisite plant as you would a treasured heirloom. When you use a single small plant, you must be very careful to see that the color of the leaves, the general shape, and the size are absolutely right for the spot in which you wish to place it—and that the plant is in the best of health.

In an old-fashioned high-ceilinged room, what could be more pleasing than the simple accents of a blooming geranium framed in the window and the small container of bleeding heart on the chest? Both plants pick up the red and pink shades of the comfortable sofa covering.

Plants as room accents

It's only natural for people to put plants on window sills or on shelves built into a window, because this gives them the best possible natural light. And while this type of display can easily be used to advantage in your decorating scheme, there are many other ways to display plants so that they have a prominent role as room accents.

One very practical alternative, and one that is exceedingly attractive as well, is to group your small plants on a serving cart. This allows you to move the cart with its entire plant grouping to a sunny window location for a part of the day, and then return it to the place in the room where you prefer it after the sun goes down. The serving cart could be made of wrought iron, wicker, or fine wood in a natural finish.

Another suggestion for displaying plants is to group them on the steps of a small library ladder. With eclectic or contemporary furnishings, you might like to take a slightly offbeat approach. Buy a small unfinished stepladder and treat it to a shiny lacquered finish in a color that complements your decor. Arrange pots of small flowering and green plants on the steps of the ladder.

During the warm months when you are not using your fireplace, don't ignore this important architectural feature. Arrange a grouping of small plants in the firebox or on the hearth in front of the fireplace. Just be sure to select plants with low light requirements as fireplace areas usually receive little light. The fireplace mantel, too, is ideal for plants with low light requirements.

Pieces of furniture made of glass or plastic, because of their crystal-clear, see-through

quality, afford excellent plant locations and the opportunity to vary from the traditional plant groupings. Place plants, interspersed with rocks, driftwood, figurines, or other small art objects, underneath a glass-topped table, inside a plastic cube table, or on the glass shelves of an étagère or a wall arrangement.

A two-story home with an open stairway provides you with a natural place to showcase your plants. If there is a landing with a window partway up the stairs, display your plants there. If there isn't a window, use a plant stand in the corner to hold one or more

Although the small den above has white walls and dark fabrics, it is a colorful and interesting room because of the brightly colored pillows, lamp bases, and the use of greens. A slim library table behind the sofa holds artifacts, an arrangement of leaves, and a feather fern.

It is hard to tell that the room at the left is furnished basically with budget, do-it-yourself furnishings because the profusion of plants contributes so much to the imaginative contemporary treatment. Small amounts of red add another lively note to the black and white color scheme.

plants. At the bottom of a curved stairway is another ideal spot for showing off your plants. Or maybe you have a long hallway that appears to stretch endlessly into the distance. Place a grouping of plants at the far end, and it will create the illusion of shortening the hall length.

Those of you who are building new homes have the added advantage of being able to make certain that plants can be placed in the best possible location—both for decorative purposes and for growing conditions. Consult with your architect when he is drawing up the plans, and ask him to include planters in locations where they will complement the room and its furnishings. This treatment is especially effective when the planter is backed by a rough-textured brick wall or a wood-paneled wall. At the same time, unless the planter is next to a window that will admit sufficient natural light, plan to install artifi-

cial lighting that is adequate to keep your plants healthy and growing.

If your rooms are small and you do not have much space for plants, cactus plants or cactus dish gardens should be of interest to you. Most varieties of cactus remain small under average home conditions, yet they do have interesting colors, patterns, and shapes. You can introduce an unusual room accent with a grouping of different varieties of cactus in individual pots. Or you can combine several varieties in a dish garden—mix different sizes, shapes, and colors.

Dish gardens can be planted with young green plants too. Include a variety of plants —different heights, leaf shapes, textures, and patterns—and arrange them according to whether the dish will be viewed from all sides or mostly from the front. Choose a container that is compatible with your furnishings and colors, and be sure it is deep enough to allow for a bottom layer of pebbles plus the soil. Most plants need at least three inches of soil for stability and root growth.

In making a dish garden be sure to combine only those plants that have similar light and water requirements.

At the left, top, a simple wooden shelf at the middle of the window holds small plants of unusual shape. All were chosen to add interest without obscuring the light. Among them are a wax plant and a donkey's tail sedum.

At the left, middle, gauzy sprengeri ferns are displayed on the mantel and a neanthe bella palm within the fireplace opening. Without being obtrusive they help warm the room and harmonize with the setting of marble and paintings.

At the left, bottom, an ugly radiator is partially concealed by a shelf above the heating unit. This is an ideal platform for plants, at least in the summer when the heat is off. If the window faces east, growing conditions are perfect.

A coleus collection is used as draperies to give privacy and shield the room from the next-door neighbor's view. Suspended at various heights and framed by vines, the plants serve as a glass curtain while thriving in the light.

Flowers as room accents

Using flowers as accents in today's room settings is one of the most satisfying ways to add color and decoration to your home. Their fragile and perishable qualities add to their beauty, making them stand out in a world where so many things are man-made and mass-produced.

Whenever you step into a room where fresh flowers are visible, you immediately sense that the occupants enjoy living. It doesn't matter whether they are garden flowers casually arranged, a florist's arrangement in a stylized design, or a single bloom in a bud vase. They all add beauty.

Flowers as decorative accents are now used much more freely than they ever have been before. Maybe you always place a floral centerpiece on your dining table when you are entertaining, but don't stop there. Use flowers in every room as often as you can. We sometimes forget how a tiny little arrangement—a few blooms and one spray of fern, for instance—in an unexpected place such as on a bedside table, an end table, or in a book shelf can add a delightfully individual air to any home. While big flower arrangements are dramatic, these miniature arrangements serve as important, welcome grace notes.

If you raise your own garden flowers, be sure to include cutting varieties that can be brought indoors throughout their blooming season. If you don't have a flower garden, buy flowers as often as you can. You don't always have to get expensive floral arrangements unless you want to. You can buy a few or as many flowers as you wish at your florist shop or greenhouse. And you will find that florists are cooperative in sharing their professional tips with you—how to arrange

flowers to suit your taste and needs and how to keep the blooms fresh as long as possible.

Not everyone has a natural aptitude for arranging flowers, but it is easy to increase your knowledge of this fine old art (see pages 112-117). Consider enrolling in a flower-arranging class. Such classes are sponsored by local garden clubs or adult-education programs in all parts of the country.

The clear flower colors that appear in the upholstery fabric, draperies, and paintings in the room at the left are restated in three different floral arrangements. Sweeping expanses of cooling white on the walls and the floor bring out the luminescence of these flower colors.

The large, casually arranged bouquet of cut flowers in a clear crystal container is in the spotlight in the room above. The red, yellow, orange, and white flowers, including many fully opened roses, add a bright note to the cool green shades of the furnishings and carpet.

The same basic rules that apply to home decorating—those concerning color, scale, and balance—hold true for flowers. The colors of flowers, their composition, and their size and shape should all relate to the surroundings in which they will be shown, and their containers should harmonize with the decor as well as the flowers.

It's not hard to learn color harmony as it is related to flowers. Choose flower colors for monochromatic, neutral, analogous, and complementary decorating schemes just as you would choose other accessories. Nature's own colors are so well done that it requires very little skill to use them effectively.

However, unlike the pigments that are man-made, flower colors are never pure. Red shades off to purple and orange to yellow in a single bloom, so you can't expect to match flowers to decorating schemes as precisely as you match paints. The various tones of white are always in good taste anywhere—no matter what colors are used in the room.

There are three styles of flower arranging —traditional, Oriental, and modern. The traditional arrangements are typically a mass of mixed flowers with the large blooms and deep hues concentrated at the center and the smaller flowers and foliage used around the outer edges to outline the basic shape of the design. These are at home with traditional or country furnishings and can be arranged equally well in tall or low containers.

In Oriental style, the emphasis is placed on line. The arrangements may be formal or informal, but in each there is a triangle. They show the Japanese genius for revealing beauty in simplicity, or, in other words, how a very few flowers can achieve a larger effect. In addition to complementing Oriental furnishings, they lend themselves well to contemporary decorating.

Modern designs stem from the Oriental style more than from the traditional style. Modern and its offshoot, abstract, are unorthodox in that, in order to create a certain mood, they sometimes let the flowers and foliage supplement the container and accessories, rather than the other way around. Just as with modern and abstract in other forms, the designer is most concerned with a personal interpretive expression. Driftwood, rocks, and sculptured pieces are often incorporated into the design along with the flowers, foliage, and container. Modern and abstract floral designs are completely in harmony with today's contemporary furnishings.

You can literally double the visual pleasure of flowers by placing them in front of a mirror that hangs above a mantel, chest of drawers, or table. Even a few flowers take on an extra dimension when they are reproduced in the mirror's silvered face.

The orange upholstered furniture in a contemporary living room is accented by the same color in the gladiolus that are combined with Scotch broom in a modern—almost Oriental—arrangement. The gentle flow of the Scotch broom is echoed by the curve of the shallow bowl.

In a living-dining room, shades of yellow, green, and white are skillfully played from one area to another. The bouquet of zinnias and its container, and the bowl of fruit, repeat the colors and add some red and pink for contrasting accents.

Decorating for the season

No matter where you live, you can use plants and flowers to give fresh meaning to each season of the year. Nature has many offerings that herald the arrival of each season in all parts of the country.

The rebirth of nature that takes place every spring takes on additional meaning when you use spring blooms, foliage, and flowering plants to decorate your home. It takes only a few blooms of tulips, daffodils, or lilacs plus a few flowering or even bare branches to make an impressive arrangement. Or use one or more of the spring-flowering bulb plants—hyacinth, narcissus, daffodil, tulip, or crocus.

What could be more exciting than a window full of plants for the Christmas season? At left, a duo of kalanchoe plants rests in a decorated wooden chest, another in an octagonal humidor. The poinsettias, azaleas, cyclamen, and Norfolk pine are set in containers decorated with decals, braids, stars, and cutouts from Christmas cards.

In the early summer a table like the one above makes any meal something special—whether it is a brunch, lunch, or dinner. The low white bowl of pink peonies and weigela establishes the color scheme for table linens, china, and even the dessert. The frivolous tablecloth is easily made out of pink and white striped cotton and the napkins are of solid matching pink.

As summer approaches, you can look forward to enjoying the luxury of using large quantities of garden flowers. There are peonies, iris, snapdragons, roses, lilies, zinnias, sweet William, nasturtiums, petunias, marigolds, and dahlias. You can bring the summer mood inside by using simple garden flowers —individually or mixed—and arranging them in luxuriantly full but casual designs.

When fall arrives, you have the many varieties of chrysanthemums. As cut flowers, they last so well that they're definitely a favorite for floral arrangements to decorate your home. Combine mums with glossy, dark green foliage for an effective grouping.

During the autumn season, when the

blooms in your garden have disappeared, look around for new materials for arrangements. Use milkweed pods, sumac, pine cones, oats, goldenrod, and other pods, weeds, and grasses. These dried materials are especially effective when they are arranged in tall vases that stand on the floor. (See pages 82-85.)

Almost before you realize it, the Christmas season is upon you. Decorate with winter's greens, pine cones, poinsettias, and other flowering plants for a festive holiday. A nice touch is to place tiny poinsettia plants on bedroom and powder room vanities.

At the left, a variety of spring-blooming bulbs is lined up on a wide windowsill. Red tulips, yellow daffodils, and purple hyacinths in clay pots add a cheerful note. Once the plants are in bloom keep them out of too much direct sunlight so as to prolong their life.

The fall arrangement above is an excellent example of the dramatic effects you can achieve with treasures from your attic or basement. An old tin pitcher contains yellow chrysanthemums, dried hydrangeas, and grasses. A wooden decoy and old prints complete the fall theme.

CHAPTER 5

Dried Arrangements and Permanent Plants and Flowers

Although a person's first love is most likely to be for live plants and freshly cut flowers, there are many occasions when dried arrangements, or permanent plants and flowers will best fill a decorating need.

Dried arrangements are natural plants that have been dried. Permanent plants and flowers are man-made, but are seldom called artificial plants or reproductions any more because they are so realistic it is difficult to tell them from their live counterparts.

There are many reasons why you might choose either of these for your decorating scheme. Dried arrangements are long lasting and can take the place of fresh flowers when the blooming season is past. Even though you

may buy cut flowers frequently throughout the year, you will find that there are many places in your home where a dried arrangement adds beauty and saves money too.

Permanent plants and flowers also have their place in home decorating. If you have difficulty controlling the temperature and light in certain areas of your home, or if you are away from home a great deal, permanent plants and flowers may be the solution for you. Then, too, they can be combined perfectly well with live plants and flowers. Perhaps you have live plants in areas where there is adequate natural light, but in addition you would like flowers on the fireplace mantel, or a house tree in a dark corner or windowless entrance hall. Here you could use permanent plants and flowers.

In this hospitable living room the dried arrangements are cued to the gold tones of the furnishings, all of which look quite handsome against the Oriental rug and walls painted in the same shade of terra-cotta. Beside the fireplace is a cast-iron plant, or aspidistra.

Dried arrangements

Dried materials have textural interest, decorative shapes, and colors that are primarily the subtle earth tones or the warm sun hues.

When the blooming season is over in your own garden, explore the woods, roadsides, marshes, and banks of ponds and lakes for materials for dried arrangements. There are weeds, grasses, slim cattails, seeds, pods, and a variety of other things you may find. It's fun to search for them too. To add to your own collection, visit your florist and see his exotic imports, such as wood roses from Hawaii, palm spathes, and lotus seedpods. Curving branches of orange bittersweet berries are a natural for autumn arrangements and combine well with other dried materials.

Dried plant life lends itself well to casual arrangements. When you choose containers for your dried arrangements, consider the color schemes in the rooms where they will be placed, and be sure that the container and its contents are scaled to the size of the room and the furnishings in it.

In making an arrangement to place on the floor, choose a tall vase. Combine long stalks of wheat, milkweed pods, cattails, and several sprays of curved bittersweet. This type of arrangement is particularly at home in an entrance hall, in a corner of a room, or beside a fireplace. Neutral vase tones bring out the autumnal colors of the dried materials. (If you have small children or pets, *remember that the bittersweet berries are poisonous and sould be displayed well out of reach.*)

Soaring stems of pussy willow, which appears early each spring, will last throughout the year and make a stunning tall arrangement. For a low shallow bowl, try a combination of hedge apples, short branches of pine, and pine cones.

In the kitchen at the left, an arrangement of dried hydrangeas is placed on the shelf above the sink where it blends with the ceramic containers. A bowl of dried, varicolored statice decorates the top of the staple and spice box.

The dried arrangements in the room above repeat the same warm tones that appear in the floor covering, painting, and other accessories. The fresh leaves in the fireplace add still another imaginative note to the overall decorating scheme.

In this entryway a compact, yet fluffy, arrangement of dried flowers and three airy green plants on unusual slender white stands add softness to the contemporary styling of the walnut-faced plywood cabinet and the mirror above it.

You can also dry your own flowers and greens for colorful winter bouquets. Goldenrod, strawflowers, cockscomb, oats, rye, leaves, seedpods, and ferns are all likely candidates for drying. You don't even need any special equipment for drying—a closet or your attic can serve as the drying room.

Timing is especially important in the gathering of materials. Flowers that are cut when they are in semibud form will open into full bloom as they dry. Gather grasses and ferns in the morning when they are fresh. Cut leaves as they start turning from green to yellow or red. Select flat branches, as they are the most easily pressed.

If you have to transport them any great distance, put the fresh materials in buckets of water. Also, the sooner you press the colored materials after they are picked, the brighter the colors will remain during the drying process. Choose a dark, dry location for the drying process. Dampness hinders proper drying, and light fades the colors. Once the flowers and leaves are dry and the colors are set, they won't fade even when placed in a sunny location.

To press leaves, lay each branch out carefully between layers of newspaper on a flat surface. Make as many layers as you like, and weight down the pile with heavy objects.

To obtain curved stems, dry part of your tall materials by standing them upright in kegs or bottles set on the floor of your drying room. Leave undisturbed until they are dry. But you will want straight stems on most materials. Tie them into bundles, hang them from the ends of the stems on lines, and let them dry three or four weeks.

Under ideal conditions, the drying process should take no longer. The dried materials are ready to use in arrangements when the flower petals feel rigid and no moisture is left in the paper layers of pressed foliage. Leaves that are not thoroughly dry when you remove them will curl and lose their shape.

Don't by any means wait until autumn to start collecting your flowers for drying. Many summer varieties, such as larkspur, ageratum, globe amaranth, stock, and zinnias, are easy to dry and hold their colors well. Cut each variety whenever it reaches its peak blooming period and hang for drying.

Weeds and cultivated plants that are suitable for drying include the following: sumac, joe-pye weed, yarrow, clover, statice, spirea, delphinium, hydrangea, vervain, tansy, salvia, bee balm, and butterfly weed.

In this den-library the rows of books are broken up by the attractive wicker baskets of orange skyrockets and beige sea oats, which tie in with the book bindings, furniture, and russet floor tiles. A permanent plant provides a touch of green, which is picked up in the jungle-motif wall covering and the bottles.

CEZANNE

CEZANNE IN FULL COLOUR

FORTUNE

Permanent flowers

Permanent flowers (or floral reproductions) were at one time taboo as far as good decorating was concerned but are now accepted in the finest decorating schemes.

There are many reasons why they have gained this stature. No longer do they have an inferior artificial appearance. The material they are made of may be synthetic, but it is so soft to the touch that it feels like a baby's skin. Or they may be made of such fabrics as silk, velvet, organdy, batiste, or chiffon. The designs are executed with such skill that it is almost impossible to detect them from live flowers. Their beauty is long lasting, and you can have the blooms of your choice regardless of the season of the year.

Very few people can afford to have live flowers that complement their decorating scheme the year around. But you can decorate with good permanent flowers in the color and variety of your choice.

If you have a knack for flower arranging, you probably will want to purchase the flowers and greens and make your own arrangements. Otherwise rely on a florist who has good floral designers on his staff who can do the job for you. If you have containers of your own—silver, copper, brass, pewter, porcelain, crystal, or earthenware—take them to your florist and discuss with him just what effect you desire. Tell him your color scheme, style of furnishings, overall decorative mood of the room, and where you would like to display the arrangements. This background information is just as necessary to your decorating plan as it would be if you were selecting a painting for your home.

One distinct advantage of using permanent flowers, other than their long-lasting quality and realistic appearance, is that you can choose exactly the color and variety that best accents your furnishings and harmonizes with the container you want to use.

The places where you are most likely to use permanent flowers are in an entrance hall, on a fireplace mantel, on a bathroom vanity, on a desk, or in bookshelves.

In most cases, you would not choose them for a dining-table centerpiece. But should you use a handsome centerpiece of permanent flowers for your dining table, tuck in just a few live flowers to add fragrance.

In the living room at the left, with its neutral beige and brown colors, the fireplace is the focal point. The painting above the mantel is flanked by silver urns filled with casual arrangements of bright orange permanent flowers.

The room above has a restful color scheme that stems from the coppery tones in the fabric covering the wall panels. The pewter pitcher holds yellow permanent flowers that blend with the subdued furnishings while adding a sunny note.

Permanent plants

There are some locations in almost every home where it is nearly impossible to keep plants growing healthily. It could be an entrance hall where the temperature changes drastically. Or it could be a corner where there is no natural light. If you have any of these problems yet want to use green plants as a decorative accent, try permanent plants.

Before you make your choice, visit a nursery or botanical garden and study the plants carefully. Then when you shop for a permanent plant you will be able to judge how realistic are the bark, leaf texture, and color. Try to duplicate the natural features as closely as possible. When using several permanent plants in a group, choose varieties that, as natural plants, have the same growing conditions. They will seem more natural.

The open gallery floor in the vacation home at the left cries for a hanging plant, yet the position of such a plant makes it hard to water, and, the owners are not regularly present to do so. A permanent kangaroo vine could be the solution, along with long-lasting rhododendron leaves and two striking dried arrangements.

The family room above, with its rough plaster and whitewashed brick walls, also needs green plants, but the room receives little light. The answer is a very impressive permanent Queensland umbrella tree, which provides exactly the right note of glossy, luxurious foliage and picks up the greens of the upholstery fabrics.

CHAPTER 6

Plant Stands, Containers, and Terrariums

It is true that in recent years plants, flowers, and dried flowers and foliage have become increasingly popular in home decorating because of their beauty, their unique ability to create a note of tranquility, and the feeling they give us of being close to the natural world. Consequently, and luckily for the homemaker, the choice of planters and containers in which to display our plants has widened enormously compared to what it was in the past.

Now it is possible to find a large range in every sort of design, color, size, and shape, and something that will go with any style or mood of our decorating schemes. You can

In this high-ceilinged room a slender black metal plant stand provides the necessary height without adding bulk. It gives the illusion that the large Boston fern, with its welcome addition of green to the predominantly red color scheme, is almost suspended in air. The lower shelves can serve as a handy occasional table.

buy planters, containers, and terrariums in florist shops, variety stores, gift shops, and supermarkets. With a bottlecutting kit you can make terrariums and containers inexpensively out of wine and other glass bottles. Also you may find that you have something at home, perhaps in the attic, which lends itself to the display of greenery and flowers.

And for those of you who want built-in planters there are many designs that can be built by the home handyman or a local craftsman. If you are in the throes of building a new home, consult with your architect or contractor in the early stages about including one or more planters in the plans. Be sure that they are built where there is adequate natural light, or else have artificial lighting built in at the same time.

Plant stands

Plant stands can be large or small, movable or built in, something you already have in your home that can be utilized or something you purchase. Before you decide what type of plant stand you want, consider the amount of space and the light that is available in the particular area where you wish to show plants, and whether you want a plant stand that is tall or short. Also choose a design that is suitable for and scaled to the size of the furnishings in the room.

Shelves of all types fall into the category of plant stands. Built-in bookshelves are excellent for showing plants, but you may have to build in artificial light or move the plants to a spot near a window during part of the day. Tall, slim étagères of shiny metal or black or painted wrought iron with glass or clear plastic shelves are also ideal. Because they will not block the view, they can even be placed in front of windows.

If you wish to place some plants where there is not enough light, why not try grouping them on a low table or bench and put casters on the table or bench? Then you can easily put them in front of a window during the day and return them to their proper place in the late afternoon.

An interesting plant stand to place at one side of an old-fashioned tall window can be made simply by giving a plain painter's ladder, shelf and all, a spanking new coat of bright colored lacquer.

There are plant stands in different sizes and designs that come equipped with light tubes and waterproof trays. All you have to do is plug them in wherever you wish. There are even ones designed for tabletops.

The étagère of bright chrome and sparkling glass shelves in the sunroom at the left serves as a stand for plants and bibelots. The plants and accessories have been chosen carefully, used sparingly, and arranged with great sophistication to maintain a light and airy feeling.

A lazy Susan plant stand is ideal for African violets, as it can easily be revolved to give the right amount of light for each plant. One like that at the left might be a do-it-yourself project with the purchase of a lazy Susan bearing post, heavy plywood for the circular shelves, and laminated plastic for the surface.

The sitting room below looks out on a magnificent garden with many trees. What is needed in the predominantly neutral white room are a few accents of green that will bring the outdoors in but not compete with it. The tall, tapering plant stand does not interfere with the view and holds just the right number of small plants.

Containers and planters

Even the simplest house plants will take on an aura of elegance when they are growing in handsome containers or planters. With the wide selection that is available in all colors, designs, sizes, and prices to suit every budget, it is possible to choose planters and containers for your house plants that will add a new dimension to your decor.

It seems as though nothing will ever completely replace the standard clay pot, for it has an earthy pink-brown color that goes perfectly with green plants. Plastic pots and Styrofoam pots are capturing a big share of the market because they are lightweight and unbreakable. Plastic pots come in assorted decorator colors and also in clear plastic which enables you to see plants growing beneath the soil. Regardless of which of these three types of pots your plants are in when you purchase them, you may want to place the pots in other decorative containers which match your decor.

To go with the natural look that is becoming more and more evident in home furnishings designs and materials, handsomely handcrafted plant containers are more in demand. There are basket containers of wicker, rattan, chestnut, and willow in sizes that are

large enough to hold a gigantic house tree or small enough for a single small plant. Hanging baskets made of these materials come with drip-proof plastic or tole liners. You can even buy hanging baskets already planted with herbs to please the gourmet cook.

Ceramic containers, both glazed and unglazed, in novel shapes, designs, and earth-tone colors, also complement the natural theme. In addition, there are metal and porcelain containers in traditional styles.

To accent contemporary furnishings and interiors, there are plant containers of plastic in both the clear see-through and opaque ver-

sions. These come in the standard flower-pot shape in clear plastic or in bright colors. Some even have individual metal holders so they can be mounted on walls and arranged in groupings. You can also buy plastic containers in cube and rectangular shapes. Or if you are a hobbyist you can make your own. Make a square container of clear plastic, line the bottom with colored marbles and a layer of moss for drainage, and then put in the plant and soil. The see-through quality will allow you to tell when the plant needs watering. (Do not put clear plastic containers in direct sun or plant roots will burn.)

In the contemporary room at the left, the graceful lines of the areca palm in the corner, the soaring lamp, and the unusual mobile put the room in motion. The palm's ceramic container is a plain white cylinder that repeats the simplicity of the design of the furniture.

The city high-rise apartment living room above, with its wall of windows, is a natural habitat for a lover of plants and flowers. The handwoven basket containers for the large plants and the simple natural clay pots for the smaller ones reflect the honest, unadorned modern style.

Planters may be a built-in architectural feature or portable. If you are building a new home or remodeling an older one, this is your chance to have one or more permanent planters. Otherwise you may be more interested in portable planters.

There are both domestic and imported planters in every conceivable kind of natural and man-made material. The Oriental influence that is making news in all forms of decoration is also showing up in planters. For example, large porcelain hibachis and antique bronze hibachis are being used for planters.

Then there are the floor planters of Siamese teakwood. These are tall and slim and will hold a group of flower pots. They are ideal for ivy, asparagus fern, and philodendron arranged in a hanging-garden effect.

From Mexico comes a great variety of both hanging and standing planters in wrought iron. These are especially suited to Mediterranean furnishings and decor.

There are urn-type planters of plastic that closely resemble the traditional stone or marble designs. They are lightweight, unbreakable, weatherproof, and inexpensive. You can find planters of wicker and willow; ones of copper, brass, and bronze; and ones of porcelain and ceramic complete with waterproof liners.

Also, you probably have some household utensils that can double as planters. An old copper wash boiler or tub, a cast-iron Dutch oven or enameled roaster, an earthenware crock or wooden keg can all be converted into conversation-piece planters.

The planter at top left is made of three wooden boxes placed together as a continuous long planter. The boxes are lined and filled with white gravel, in which the pots are sunk. A line of Boston ferns mixed with other plants of increasing height builds to the Java fig at the end.

The cedar planter at bottom left is versatile. A magnificent lacy tree philodendron is placed in one section while squares of ceramic tiles cover the other two. The tile covers are ideal for shorter plants such as these feather ferns but may be removed for other arrangements.

At the right are three shallow modular trays on bases that rest on the floor in the plant area. These pebble-filled planters and the potted plants themselves can both be shifted around in various flexible arrangements. At the moment one blooming plant and some smaller green ones have a backdrop of a Queensland umbrella tree, an evergreen grape, and a Madagascar dragon tree.

In the contemporary master bedroom-sitting room below, the fireplace hearth is converted to a pebbled planter during the summer months and affords the same space for greenery as more conventional fireplaces. Starting with the handsome fiddleleaf fig, the eye is led to the Madagascar dragon tree, the Norfolk pine, and then to the flowers on the deck outside.

Terrariums

A tiny garden of growing plants has an irresistible fascination for people of all ages. For a child, a terrarium can provide his first experience of watching a miniature garden grow and change. For an adult, it affords an opportunity to grow small plants under conditions similar to those in a greenhouse. You can use your own creativity and duplicate a scene from nature on a miniature scale.

Since moist air is trapped within the terrarium, the plants' growth is not impeded by the dry, hot air in homes and apartments in the winter. Terrariums seldom need watering because the moisture is so well conserved.

There are many types of containers that can be used for terrariums—brandy snifters, glass bowls, aquariums, and glass jars of all sizes. Or you can make your own, of glass and wood or of plastic. All terrariums should have covers. If yours does not have a glass lid,

you can improvise one of see-through plastic wrap or a sheet of glass or plastic cut to fit the opening. The cover is used to control the humidity. If moisture has condensed noticeably on the inside of the terrarium, remove the cover for a day or leave it partially uncovered until the moisture disappears.

You can display terrariums on tables, credenzas, bookshelves, window sills, or plant stands. Choose a design that harmonizes with your furnishings, and a size that is scaled to the area where it will be displayed.

The ideal plants for terrariums are those that require high humidity and grow slowly. Among those that are recommended are small-sized ferns, mosses, trailing arbutus, small philodendrons, ivies, partridgeberries, peperomias, and fittonias.

The charming, small, and well-planted terrarium at top right is the result of the twin talents of a handyman and a gardener. It is made from the beveled windows of an old door which are set into a wooden base.

It's fun to plant your own terrarium and the glass candy jar at the right is perfect. Some good soil, a bit of gravel under the soil for drainage, and infrequent watering will keep small, slow-growing plants healthy for months.

The terrarium at the bottom right is actually a discarded aquarium planted with a variety of small and young plants. Baby's tears are used as ground cover; at the left rear are a variety of palm and two young ferns; at the right are an infant podocarpus and an infant staghorn fern.

The large, widemouthed glass fruit jar at the left resting on a wooden stand makes an intriguing display case for a terrarium that is planted with a collection of tiny ferns and woodland plants. A generous sprinkling of red partridgeberries, tiny stones of contrasting shades, and shreds of old wood adds to the natural look.

CHAPTER 7

Flowers and Foliage for Tables

Flowers and greens attractively arranged in appropriate containers provide the perfect decorative touch for tables. But it does take some planning in order to show them off to the best advantage.

The size of the arrangement should be scaled to the size of the table. The color and texture of the materials and the design you choose should be compatible with the style and colors of your furnishings.

Although your first impulse may be to place an arrangement of flowers and foliage in the center of your dining table, remember that flowers are also handsome additions to

A mass of yellow daisies arranged casually in a bowl set in a wicker basket highlights this colorful dinner table. The tablecloth is made from an Indian cotton bedspread. The Mexican tinware service plates, the wooden candelabra, and the tall plants in the background emphasize the casual country atmosphere.

any table in your home. Don't neglect coffee or cocktail tables, lamp tables, bedside tables, serving tables, and patio tables. Use flowers wherever they fit.

Having a flower garden of your own gives you the distinct advantage of being able to use flowers lavishly, and you can experiment with a variety of arrangements for tables throughout your home.

When the blooming season is past, or if you don't have a garden, you must count on a florist shop or greenhouse. You can buy cut flowers and arrange them yourself, or you can order floral arrangements in the designs of your choice for your tables. If you have vases, bowls, and pitchers that you especially like, take them to the florist. He'll be happy to use whatever you ask him to.

101

Formal table settings

There's nothing like fresh flowers to add a festive note to a sit-down dinner party. Traditionally, the logical choice for such a dinner, at which the guests are seated along both sides of the table and the host and hostess at either end, is a symmetrical arrangement. Flowers arranged in this fashion should be designed so that they are attractive from every angle. And the centerpiece should be low enough so that guests can engage in across-the-table conversation. If you are unsure about the height, sit down at the table and test it.

Plan your arrangement so that it harmonizes with the rest of your table setting. Do not feel that it is the expense of the flowers that counts. Instead, it is how they contribute to the overall effect. Rather than lavishness, it is better if the whole composes into a simple, dignified effect.

Long-stemmed red roses are centered on the table in the formal dining room at the left. They are not meant to be there while dining, but they add the right touch to the color scheme when the table is not set. The Medici colors of red and blue enhance this interpretation of the classic Italian Renaissance style.

Flowers can do all sorts of marvelous things and here is an example of how only a few can add just the right amount of color. A low bowl of yellow daffodils, along with yellow ramekins and chartreuse napkins, contrast happily with the neutral black and white in the traditional dining room above. The bold wall covering sets the pace and the white shag carpeting adds texture.

Informal table settings

When it comes to decorating dining tables with flowers and foliage in an informal or casual setting, there simply are no limits. You can make these table decorations as simple or as festive as you wish, regardless of whether you have large masses of freshly cut flowers or only a few blooms.

The one important thing to remember is to coordinate the table decorations with your table settings and furnishings. Think first about the color or combinations of colors when you select the flowers for your table. It's up to you to decide what effect you wish to create—whether you want the flowers to match, harmonize with, or contrast with the colors of your china, crystal, silver, and lin-

ens. Always consider the color of flowers as the whole effect, never part of a last-minute after-thought.

And if you can, don't reserve flowers just for those occasions when you entertain. Use them as frequently as you are able to for your own family's pleasure.

With informal and casual table settings, re-member that every single thing on your table does not have to match exactly. Some of the most exciting settings are designed deliber-ately to combine different patterns and colors of tableware and linens. This does take a little skillful planning in order to create a pleasing effect—one that has a coordinated look, rather than a thrown-together appearance.

Flowers and masses of green plants help to cre-ate an indoor-outdoor decor in the dining room at the left. White director's chairs dressed in black vinyl are teamed with a sleek black marble-topped table. The bright chrysanthemums and candles add sparkle to this subdued color scheme.

A garland of orange flowers and greens stretches the length of the dining table in the contempo-rary room above, and restates the colors in the abstract painting and the cushions on the chairs. The T-square simplicity of the table contrasts with the curvilinear lines of the chairs.

Another method of getting greater variety into your table decorations is to reflect the different seasons of the year.

In the spring, use flowers with soft pastel colors—the pale blues, yellows, lavenders, and pinks. In addition to using a single pastel tint in a table centerpiece, you can combine several hues for a mixed arrangement of spring flowers. The spring-flowering bulbs—tulips, hyacinths, and daffodils—are ideal candidates that fairly radiate a breath-of-spring air. Also combine spring blooms and the foliage of flowering bulbs, shrubs, and trees to create striking table decorations. A few tulips mixed with stalks of flowering plum make a delightful combination, as do small branches of flowering crab apple with daffodils, and lilacs mixed with tulips.

As summer approaches, table settings become more casual and reflect the carefree mood of the season. But just because you eat many of your meals on the patio, the balcony, the porch, or at poolside doesn't mean you have to relinquish flowers on the table.

Pastels are still popular during the summer, but so are the vivid hues. The hot reds, pinks, and golds of zinnias, cockscomb, geraniums, marigolds and nasturtiums are best in hot weather, and if you add lots of green foliage it will act as a coolant.

Even a picnic meal served on a sturdy redwood picnic table takes on a gala spirit when the table is decked with a bold striped runner and pottery tableware that are highlighted by garden flowers in a riot of color nestling in a copper jug.

A comfortable mix of nationalities in the country furniture blends compatibly in the dining room at the left. The large casual arrangement of colorful garden flowers and the lacy tree philodendron strengthen the informal look.

Masses of green plants and a basket of red zinnias provide a brilliant contrast to the monochromatic yellow color scheme that was chosen to enlarge the small dining room above. The plants and flowers are amplified by their reflection in the mirror, which makes the room seem larger, too.

In the autumn of the year, there is probably nothing so versatile or so hardy as chrysanthemums for table centerpieces. Choose your container and type of design to complement the variety of mum you are using. Cut the stems to the length you want in your design, and remove the leaves that will be immersed in water. Crush the ends of the woody stems with a hammer so the flowers will absorb water easily. This treatment will extend the life of your mum arrangement.

Also in the fall you can make unusual arrangements with seedpods, weeds, and grasses of various forms, colors, and textures.

The poolside indoor-outdoor room above, with its generous plantings and gray-green floors and woodwork, makes a cool green retreat for a summer luncheon. To this the casually arranged garden flowers bring a note of bright, unexpected color, and so does the potted geranium blooming brightly underneath the glass-topped table.

You don't always need flowers for an exciting centerpiece, nor is it always necessary to center it. At the right, on a small table set for three is a bowl of privet against a mirrored wall, which leaves the center of the table free and reinforces the monochromatic color scheme.

Fresh flowers can be used to decorate tables in so many ways, and can be combined with many other materials, for special effects. Once you develop the skill of combining colors and controlling the scale and proportion in table decorations, you can experiment with designs that are truly your own.

Instead of the traditional centerpiece of flowers, you might like to have a small container with only a few short-stemmed blooms at each individual place setting. Just a few daisies, three dainty rosebuds, or even a single carnation in a tiny, low container can add a festive touch that makes even the simplest kind of meal a gourmet delight.

If you are serving buffet style, you have more leeway as far as the height of your flowers is concerned, since guests will not sit around one large table. And if the serving table is against a wall, the arrangement need not be attractive from every angle, as it will be viewed from the front only.

The right containers are almost as important as the flowers themselves. As you develop your flower-arranging skill, you will want to expand your collection of bowls and vases. Try to accumulate a variety of sizes and shapes. They can be made of pottery, porcelain, crystal, glass, copper, brass, silver, bronze, or pewter. And look around for household items such as pitchers, mugs, jugs, and casseroles that can double as flower holders. Wicker and woven baskets, too, make great containers for vases.

Also collect rocks, shells, and pieces of driftwood to accompany your arrangements.

Other tables

There are many types of tables other than dining tables that lend themselves to the display of greenery and flowers. There are end tables, cocktail tables, coffee tables, occasional tables, bedside tables, lamp tables, and dressing tables. In every room are tables that fill a specific need.

They may be made of wood, glass, metal, plastic, or wicker, or a combination of two or more of these materials. It doesn't matter whether they are large or small, square, round, oval, or hexagonal, high or low. You can always find room for at least one small plant or a bud vase with a single bloom. Many tables are large enough to hold a mass of flowers or a grouping of potted plants.

Small tables afford a showcase for displaying your most precious accessories, but include some greenery or flowers with them.

At the left above are just a few long-stemmed daisies in a slender vase on a cylindrical wicker table in a reading corner. This seemingly simple arrangement is scaled to the size of the grouping and provides height to balance the original and functional magazine rack.

The room at the left, with large background areas in neutral white and a predominantly blue and yellow color scheme in floor covering and upholstery fabrics, has impressive greenery. The bright yellow and white flowers on the cocktail table accentuate the white and the yellow.

In the modernized farmhouse living room above right, purple, yellow, and white flowers on the purple Parsons table, plus the green plants, intensify the color scheme. Bright blues, greens, and purples dominate, and the white sofa and the steerhide rug add to the room's rural charm.

At the right, the round table skirted to the floor in the corner window area of an old-fashioned bedroom is dramatized by a compact arrangement of small red zinnias and an exactly matching single drapery. Other red accents appear in this predominantly white and black color scheme.

Design and technique in flower arranging

There are almost no hard and fast rules that must be adhered to in flower arranging, but there are a few basic principles just as there are in all other areas of design. Use these fundamentals to guide you and you will feel more confident when you follow your own creative impulses in your designs.

Proportion: A flower arrangement is in good proportion when it appears to be just the right size for the container holding it. If you are using a tall vase, the general rule of thumb is for the height of the flowers and foliage that extend above the rim to be two and a half to three times the height of the vase. The standard height rule for arrangements in low containers is that the tallest stem should at least equal the width or diameter of the bowl.

As you become more expert in all styles of flower arranging and gradually develop your own skills, you will eventually learn to ignore these rules. Through continued practice, you will gain a sense of proportion.

Symmetry: We tend to regard flower arrangements as well balanced when they give the viewer an appearance of stability—that is, when they do not seem lopsided.

There are two kinds of balance—symmetrical and asymmetrical. Symmetrical balance is based on a vertical line drawn down the middle between two halves that are nearly identical. Asymmetrical balance has two vertical portions that are not of the same size but have equal weight and importance to the eye.

Symmetrical balance is relatively easy to achieve. Asymmetrical balance requires greater skill, but it is more rewarding to the flower arranger and is a far happier balance for contemporary and eclectic decors.

Texture: It's easy to secure contrasting textures in floral arrangements by taking advantage of nature's own contrasts. Combine soft, velvety flowers such as roses with shiny foliage like the magnolia leaves of the South. Or try mixing the rather coarse, ruffled petals of spider chrysanthemums with delicate ferns. Even more interesting contrasts can be achieved by combining dried materials with flowers. For example, use pussy willows with daffodils to capture the essence of spring in one bouquet.

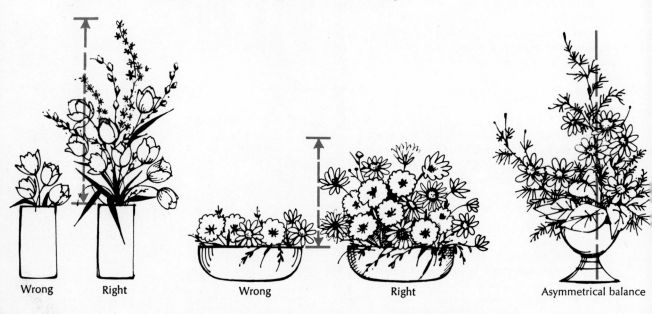

Wrong   Right   Wrong   Right   Asymmetrical balance

Floral texture can also be played up by a contrasting vase—lilacs or snapdragons in a smooth white container from Japan or Scandinavia, iris or lilies in an ornate antique vase.

Shape: Contrasting shapes, such as a rounded bloom and a pointed leaf, enhance each other when they are placed together. Deeply cut leaves give a much more interesting appearance when they are combined with solid-looking flower heads. Often the flower's own foliage will provide sufficient contrast, as it does with tulips. If it doesn't, use other types of foliage that give the necessary contrast.

Color: Color contrast within a floral arrangement is accomplished by combining hues of greater and lesser value. Dark shades look more beautiful in a low arrangement, as they appear heavier to the eye. Light tints can be used well in tall, stately arrangements. If you need additional help in choosing flowers to create the right color contrast within a room's decorating scheme, see the chapter on color, starting on page 7.

Harmony: Floral arrangements are basically harmonious when all of the elements are well blended. This is your final goal in arranging

flowers beautifully. It is the result of making a skillful selection of plant materials and containers, and arranging them in such a manner that they appear to belong together.

If you are careful to blend all of these elements together effectively, the outcome will be a satisfying design and will constitute a harmonious whole. The sketches on these pages point out the elements that add up to good design.

Not everyone is born with an instant, natural flair for arranging flowers, but a little practice can make all the difference. The most important thing is to learn to work with flowers and feel at ease with them. Do not let yourself be frightened or stiff when you arrange them. The more you handle flowers, the more you learn what each kind can and cannot do. And always let the flowers inspire and direct your arrangement.

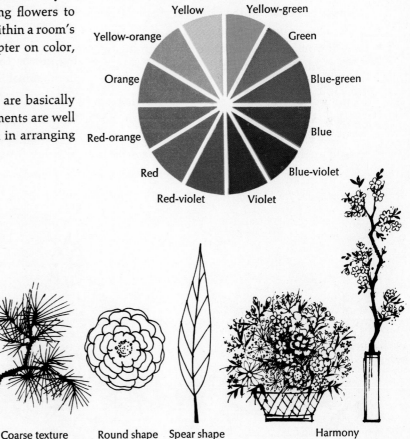

Yellow Yellow-green Green Blue-green Blue Blue-violet Violet Red-violet Red Red-orange Orange Yellow-orange

Symmetrical balance   Smooth texture   Coarse texture   Round shape   Spear shape   Harmony

Basic shapes for arrangements

The illustrations at the bottom of these pages represent the basic designs for flower arrangements. All types of arrangements, other than the Oriental or abstract designs, tend to fall into one of these categories. All of them can be classified as either mass or line designs.

When you arrange flowers, choose one of these shapes as a guide. The kind of flower and foliage you select will influence your choice of design. Some flowers lend themselves to tall arrangements; others do not. The placement of the arrangement is another factor—whether it will be displayed in a tall container that will rest on the floor, in a low bowl in the center of the dining table, on a buffet where it will be viewed from only one angle, or on a low cocktail table where it will be viewed from all sides. And don't forget that the size and shape of the arrangement must be scaled to the size and shape of the container you plan to use.

If you are a beginner at flower arranging, you will find it simpler to arrive at a successful floral arrangement by starting with a definite design in mind rather than having no plan. With continued practice, you can advance your skills and gain the confidence that will enable you to deviate from these basic forms and create arrangements that are beautiful and truly creative.

Triangular shape: This is a popular basic shape for symmetrical arrangements of traditional or contemporary style. It lends itself easily to many variations of height and width. First you must establish the lines of height and width, usually with flowers or foliage of finer form or paler color.

Next establish a focal point by placing your larger or darker-colored flowers at the center and just above the rim of the vase.

Then fill in with blooms of varied stem lengths, grouping the colors rather than scattering them about in a haphazard fashion.

Circular shape: Arranging flowers in a circular design adds an interesting element of repetition that is pleasing to the viewer's eye. You can avoid a feeling of monotony by using greens that offer a pleasant contrast to the dominant round forms.

Crescent shape: The crescent shape is an appealing line design that is asymmetrical. It is rather formal and usually appeals to those

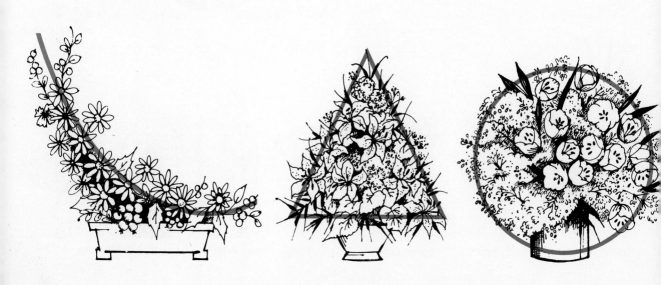

with esoteric or exotic tastes. Its execution requires more skill and experience than most of the massed arrangements.

When you select your plant materials, be sure to choose those that are pliable enough to permit manipulation. Avoid those with brittle stems, such as iris or gladiolus, as they are likely to snap when you try to bend them to the desired crescent-shaped curve.

Perpendicular line: Where you have a limited amount of display space for a flower arrangement, the perpendicular line may be just the right one. Although many tall plant materials are adaptable to this type of arrangement, gladiolus and their own spear-shaped leaves are ideal for this.

Hogarth curve: This design is named for the English artist William Hogarth, an eighteenth-century painter, who once signed a self-portrait with his name, a palette containing an S-curve like the one below, and the words "line of beauty."

The rhythmic line that distinguishes the Hogarth curve is easiest to achieve with vines or pliable branches of needled evergreen, using flowers to fill in at the center of the curve and just above and below the rim of the container. This graceful style of line ar-

rangement is a flower-show favorite.

Convex curve: This design is especially effective when designing flowers for the center of the dining table. The convex curve design is symmetrical and can be viewed from any angle. This is an important consideration for a dining-table centerpiece that must be attractive from all sides. A flower arrangement that follows the convex curve shape does not need to be tall to be attractive. For a dining table a low arrangement is especially important, as it won't interfere with conversation across the table.

Right-angle triangle: Right-angle triangular-shaped flower arrangements may face right or left, according to the location you have selected for displaying the design. Floral arrangements in right-angle triangles are especially appealing to modern arrangers because of their striking asymmetry. If your right-angle-triangle arrangement is to be seen from more than one side or will be reflected in a mirror, be sure to turn it around as you work on it, so that you can make sure both views will be equally attractive when it is finished.

This type of arrangement is usually most attractive when it is displayed in a low rectangular-shaped container.

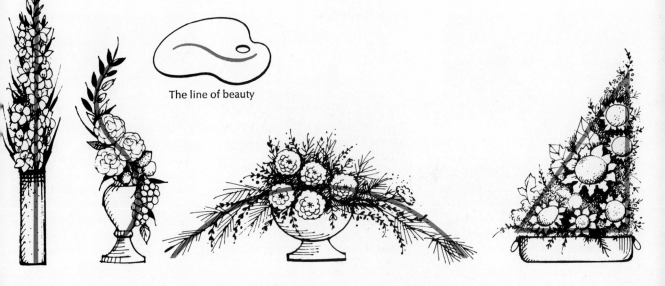

The line of beauty

Professional tips to improve arrangements

Best way to carry cut flowers from the garden is in heads-down position. Heavy-headed flowers won't snap off.

Lay flowers flat, wrap in newspaper. Plunge bunch into tepid water for 3 to 5 hours or overnight to condition.

To revive wilting flowers, snip off a half-inch of stem under water and plunge in container of tepid water.

Shape leaf to resemble its original proportions when you must trim away a brown spot along its margins.

Never place a finished arrangement where it will be exposed to draft from a fan or window, or to full sunlight.

To repair the bent stem of a heavy-headed bloom, insert toothpick to run through center and down into stem.

Many flowers and foliage stems are quite pliable and can be curved by placing thumbs together and bending.

Keeping or reviving woody stems depends on prompt pounding of bottom 2 inches before plunging in water.

To insure lavish intake of water by woody stems, pare off bark from bottom 2 inches and crosscut stems.

Cutting and preparing flowers

Flower	When to cut and how to treat
Anemone	½ to fully open. Scrape stems.
Aster	¾ to fully open. Scrape stems.
Azalea	Bud to fully open. Scrape and crush stems.
Bachelor's-button	½ to fully open. Scrape stems.
Bleeding heart	4 or 5 florets open. Scrape stems.
Buddleia	¾ to fully open. Scrape stems or sear in flame.
Calendula	Fully open. Scrape stems.
Carnation	Fully open; snap or break from plant. Scrape stems.
Canna	½ to fully open. Scrape stems.
Chrysanthemum	Fully open. Break off and scrape or crush stems.
Clematis	¾ to fully open. Scrape stems.
Daffodil	As color shows in bud. Cut foliage sparingly or bulb will not mature. Scrape stems.
Dahlia	Fully open. Sear stems in flame.
Daisy	½ to fully open. Scrape stems or sear in flame.
Day lily	¾ to fully open. Flowers last just one day.
Delphinium	¾ to fully open. Scrape stems; snap off top buds.
Geranium	Fully open. Scrape stems.
Gerbera	¾ to fully open. Sear stems in flame.
Gladiolus	As second floret opens. Scrape stems; snap off top buds.
Heliotrope	¾ to fully open. Sear stems in flame.
Hollyhock	¾ to fully open. Float florets or scrape stems.
Hydrangea	Fully open. Sear stems in flame.
Iris	As first bud opens. Do not cut foliage; scrape stems.
Larkspur	¾ to fully open. Scrape stems; snap off top buds.
Lilac	½ to fully open. Scrape and crush stems; float wilted branches in 110-degree water for an hour.
Lily	As first bud opens. Cut no more than ⅓ of stem or bulb will not mature. Scrape stems.
Marigold	Fully open. Scrape stems.
Mignonette	¾ to fully open. Sear stems in flame.
Morning-glory	In evening when closed. Wrap each bud in soft paper; sear vine stem; let stand in deep water overnight.
Narcissus	As color shows. Cut foliage sparingly; scrape stems.
Nasturtium	½ to fully open. Use with its own foliage.
Peony	Bud in color to fully open. Scrape or split stems.
Poinsettia	Full color. Sear stems and points from which leaves have been removed.
Poppy	Night before opening. Sear stems; drop of wax in heart of flower keeps it open.
Rose	As second petal unfurls. Cut stem just above a five-petal leaf or plant will stop blooming. Scrape stems.
Snapdragon	¾ to fully open. Scrape stems; snap off top buds.
Stock	¾ to fully open. Scrape stems; snap off top buds.
Sweet pea	¾ to fully open. Snap stem from vine.
Tulip	Bud to ½ open. Cut foliage sparingly; scrape stems. Wrap flowers in paper; stand in deep water overnight.
Violet	½ to fully open. "Harden" by soaking in water for half-hour, then wrap and refrigerate.
Water lily	Tight bud. Sear stems in boiling water; drop of wax in heart of flower keeps it open.
Zinnia	Fully open. Sear stems in flame.

One end of a family room has been transformed into a greenhouse for showing plants. Sliding glass doors separate it from the living area so temperature and humidity can be controlled. When spotlighted at night, the greenhouse becomes the most important decorating element in the room and a dazzling display from outside.

CHAPTER 8

Tips on Growing Healthy Plants

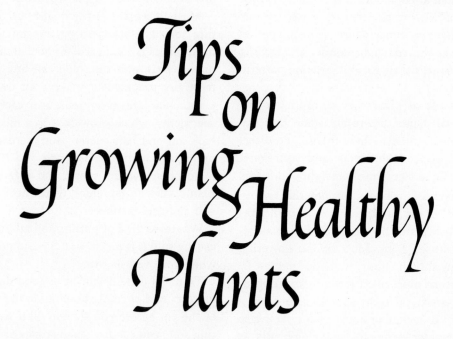

As much attention must be given to the care of plants as to their decorative aspects. Unless they are healthy, they won't be a striking addition to your decor.

Watering and feeding house plants are a never-ending topic for conversation, and the correct answers depend on so many variables. For example, during the winter months, when your home or apartment is warm and dry, your plants will need more frequent watering than during warm, humid summer weather. Also, plants in large pots do not need watering as often as those in small pots, because those in small pots dry out faster. Flowering plants need more water when they are in bloom than at other times. Except for cactus and succulents, most plants grow best in soil that is evenly moist.

A good rule to follow is to water plants whenever the surface feels dry. This could be once a day or it could be only once a week. Water them thoroughly, so that the water moistens the soil all the way from the top to the bottom of the pot.

If you water from the top, be sure to have pebbles or other loose material at the bottom of the pot to ensure good drainage. For most plants other than cactus and succulents, it's almost impossible to overwater provided you have excellent drainage.

Pebbles are not necessary when watering plants from the bottom. Instead, insert a wick (preferably one of fiber glass) to absorb the water from a dish below, which will keep the soil moist.

Overfeeding is a common mistake that many beginning gardeners make. Whatever type of plant food you use, remember that a little goes a long way but too much can burn the roots and actually kill plants. The amount of food your plants need is also influenced by the season of the year. While older plants thrive on a light feeding every few weeks, it is best to stop feeding them during the winter months unless they are flowering plants that are in bloom at this time. Most of the nonflowering plants used as decorations in the home go into a reduced growing period during the short daylight months, and feeding them disturbs their natural growing pattern.

Light needs of plant vary according to the individual plants. There are some that can be grown in rooms where there is no direct light, such as aspidistras and sanseveria species. Others need medium light or diffused light—next to a window, but one that is covered with sheer curtains if it is a south window. Such plants as ferns and begonias require diffused light. Most of the flowering plants need high light.

More and more plant enthusiasts are turning to artificial light in order to have a healthier collection of house plants. This also allows greater leeway in displaying plants, as the artificial light can be used anywhere in the home. Your artificial lighting arrangement can be as simple or as sophisticated as you desire. Just one small plant under a table lamp is a start. If an incandescent bulb is used, it should be at least 75 watts and should be placed no farther than four feet above the foliage and no closer than two feet. Fluorescent tubes can be as close as six or eight inches from the plants because they are cool.

You can buy units that come equipped with light tubes and waterproof plant trays. All you have to do is plug them in wherever you please. Or you may want to design and build one of your own to fit in a certain area in your home—in bookshelves or below the hanging cabinets in the kitchen.

Growing flowering and foliage plants under artificial light has created a whole new world of indoor gardening possibilities.

Potting and repotting plants are not difficult to do, but there are a few simple rules to fol-

low to ensure healthy plant growth.

Most important is the quality of the potting soil. The standard potting mixture for most plants is composed of equal amounts of gravel, peat, and soil. You can buy it commercially prepared or make your own. The plants that are exceptions are: cactus and succulents, which grow best in a mixture of half soil and half coarse sand; ferns, which prefer a mixture of half soil and half leaf mold or sphagnum moss; and a few house plants, such as gardenias, which need an acid soil and acid fertilizer.

Whatever kind of potting soil mixture you use, be sure it is moist—not dry and not wet—when you are using it.

To make certain you have good drainage, place a layer of coarse material in the bottom of the pot before you start to fill it with potting soil. You can use small stones or broken chunks of clay pots for this. If you use a self-watering pot, you can omit this step.

Consider the appearance, too, when you pot a plant. Choose a pot that is the correct size—that is, one that is in proportion to the size of the plant. If the plant is young and you expect it to grow rapidly, allow for this growth when you choose the size of the pot or you will have to repot again soon.

Check your plants every few months to see whether they should be repotted. A plant needs repotting when the roots become matted all around the outside of the soil ball in which it is growing.

In most cases, it is best to shift a plant to a pot no more than one or two inches larger than the one it was in. If the pot is too large in relation to the size of the plant, the soil will dry out very slowly and it will be difficult to control the moisture.

Usually you can simply add fresh potting soil at the bottom, sides, and top of the new pot, and set the plant you have just removed from its old pot, with its roots undisturbed, into the larger pot. Thoroughly water all newly potted plants and set them in a spot where they will receive light, but not bright sunlight, for several days after they have been repotted.

Keeping plants watered when you are away from home can be accomplished in different ways. If you water them thoroughly and encase the entire plants in plastic "tents," leaving some gaps for air circulation, you can keep most plants supplied with moisture for about two weeks. Insert stakes to keep the plastic from touching the foliage, and move the plants away from direct sunlight.

Or you can "double." Set the pots in other pots several sizes larger and pack the space in between with well-dampened sphagnum. This too will keep average plants in good condition for a period of two weeks.

When you plan to be gone from home for more than two weeks, arrange for someone to come in and water your plants at specified times. There are even plant-sitting services in some areas where you can hire specialists to care for your plants. Or in the case of large and costly plants or house trees, you can have them picked up and cared for in a greenhouse during your absence.

Caring for gift plants properly can extend their blooming period. It's not reasonable to expect flowering plants to live on indefinitely, as do many nonflowering plants, but you can enjoy their beauty as long as possible if you follow a few simple rules.

Many blooming gift plants cannot bloom or live a long period of time outside of the greenhouse conditions they are accustomed to. Therefore they need special attention to survive in the desertlike atmosphere that is prevalent in most homes in the winter.

With only a few exceptions (listed below), seasonal blooming plants will last longest in your home when they are placed in a cool, light, but not sunny location and given ample water at room temperature. If you place your gift plant in a watertight container, check on the drainage, as the roots will usually rot if the pot stands in water.

The suggestions that follow are for plants whose needs vary from those of most varieties of gift plants.

1. *Azaleas.* The varieties sold as florists' pot plants may not be hardy in your climate. If they are, plant them outdoors in a suitable shaded location early in the spring. Be sure to water them regularly.

2. *Bulb plants.* When hyacinths, daffodils, and crocuses are in bloom, keep them out of sunlight. When blooms fade, move them to a cool window; continue to water. When the ground softens, plant them in the garden.

3. *Christmas begonias.* This winter-blooming hybrid used to be a fragile plant, but recently it has been greatly improved. If you take good care of this gift, the lovely white flowers can continue to bloom until Easter—even in our typically overheated rooms.

4. *Cyclamens.* These plants need sun in order to continue blooming. The buds will push up and bloom provided they are in a cool, sunny window and get ample water.

5. *Holly bushes.* If these are hardy in your climate, set them outdoors in the early spring. Give them partial shade and water frequently. If they are not hardy in your area, keep yours as pot plants in a cool, sunny place, with ample water and high humidity.

6. *Poinsettias.* In a cool but sunny window, with daily watering, good drainage, and a room humidity of at least 30 percent, you may be able to prolong the life of a Christmas poinsettia plant so that it is still attractive at Easter time.

Growing requirements for foliage house plants

Foliage Plants	Normal Size	Light Requirement	Water Requirement
Aluminum Plant	6 in.	High	Moist
Caladium	to 2 ft.	Medium	Moist
Cast-Iron Plant	18 in.	Medium	Moist
Coleus	to 3 ft.	Very high	Moist
Croton	to 6 ft.	High	Moist/dry
Dieffenbachia	to 4 ft.	Low	Moist/dry
Dracaena Fragrans (Cornstalk Plant)	to 10 ft. or more	Medium	Moist
Dracaena Draco (Madagascar Dragon Tree)	to 10 ft.	Medium	Moist
Asparagus Fern (Sprengeri Fern)	to 6 ft. (hanging)	Medium	Moist
Boston Fern (Sword Fern)	2 ft.	Medium	Moist
Feather Fern	2 ft.	Medium	Moist
Fiddleleaf Fig	to 20 ft.	Medium	Moist
Weeping Fig	to 20 ft.	High	Moist
Goldfish Plant	1 ft. (hanging)	Medium	Moist
Devil's Ivy	to 5 ft. (trailing)	Low	Dry
English Ivy	5 ft. (climbing or trailing)	Low	Moist
Grape Ivy	2 ft. (hanging)	Low	Moist
Pittsburgh Ivy	1 ft. (trailing)	Medium	Moist
Jade Tree Plant	3 ft.	Low	Moist/dry
Kangaroo Vine	2 ft. (trailing)	Low	Moist
Monstera	to 5 ft.	Medium	Moist/dry
Norfolk Pine	to 7 ft.	Low	Moist
Areca Palm	10 ft.	Medium	Moist

Foliage Plants	Normal Size	Light Requirement	Water Requirement
Fern Palm	to 12 ft.	Low	Moist
Neanthe Bella Palm	3 ft.	Low	Moist
Parlor Palm	2½ ft.	Low	Moist
Peperomia	8 to 10 in.	Medium	Moist/dry
Heart-Leaf Philodendron	2 ft. or more (climbing)	Medium	Moist/dry
Lacy-Tree Philodendron	12 ft. (spreading)	Medium	Moist/dry
Piggyback Plant	18 in. (best hanging)	Low	Moist
Prayer Plant (Nerve Plant)	12 to 18 in.	Medium	Moist/dry
Podocarpus	to 5 ft.	Low	Moist
Rubber Plant	4 to 5 ft.	Low	Moist/dry
Schefflera	to 20 ft.	Low	Moist/dry
Donkey's Tail Sedum	to 18 in. (hanging)	Very high	Dry
Silver Evergreen	1 ft.	Low	Dry
Snake Plant	to 18 in.	Low	Moist/dry
Spider Plant	18 in. (hanging)	Medium	Moist
Ti Plant	2 ft.	Medium	Moist
Umbrella Plant	4 to 7 ft.	Medium	Moist
Wandering Jew	2 ft. (hanging)	High	Moist/dry
Wax Plant	7 ft. (hanging or climbing)	Medium	Moist/dry

Light Requirement

Low—amount of daylight is not enough to read by
MEDIUM—readable daylight but no direct sun
HIGH—an east or north window area receiving two hours sun daily (or north window is unobstructed)
VERY HIGH—a window area receiving more than a half-day of direct sun

Water Requirement

DRY—soil becomes moderately dry between watering almost to bottom of container
MOIST/DRY—soil is evenly moist *but not wet;* then allow to dry about one-half the depth of container
MOIST—soil is quite moist and is never allowed to dry out

Growing requirements for flowering house plants

Flowering House Plants	Normal Size	Light Requirement	Water Requirement
African Violet	4 to 5 in.	High/very high	Moist
*Agapanthus	to 3 ft.	High	Moist
Aloe	to 1 ft.	High	Moist/dry
*Amaryllis	2 ft. or more	High	Moist/dry
Aphelandra	3 ft.	Medium	Moist
Azalea	9 to 12 in.	Very high	Moist
*Begonia (tuberous)	7 to 9 in.	Very high	Moist
Browallia	1 ft. (hanging)	Medium	Moist
Calamondin Orange	9 to 19 in.	High	Moist/dry
Chenille Plant	11 in. to 2 ft.	High	Moist
*Christmas Cactus	6 to 7 in.	High	Moist
Christmas Kalanchoe	6 to 12 in.	Very high	Dry
Chrysanthemum	8 to 20 in.	Very high	Moist/dry
*Clivia	1 to 2 ft.	Medium	Moist/dry
*Crocus	5 to 7 in.	Very high	Moist
Crown of Thorns	9 to 15 in.	Very high	Moist
*Cyclamen	12 to 14 in.	Medium	Moist
*Daffodil	15 to 18 in.	Very high	Moist
Flowering Maple	to 10 ft.	High	Moist
Fuchsia	2 ft. (hanging)	Medium	Moist
Gardenia	1 ft. or more	Very high	Moist

Flowering House Plants	Normal Size	Light Requirement	Water Requirement
Geranium	8 to 15 in.	Very high	Dry
*Gloxinia	12 to 18 in.	Very high	Moist
*Grape Hyacinth	6 in.	Very high	Moist
*Hyacinth	13 in.	Very high	Moist
Hydrangea	15 to 20 in.	Medium	Moist
Jerusalem Cherry	to 2 ft.	Very high	Moist
*Narcissus	10 to 18 in.	Very high	Moist
Pepper Plant	15 in.	Medium	Moist/dry
*Poinsettia	12 to 20 in.	Very high	Moist
*Primrose	7 to 14 in.	Medium	Moist

Key for Growing Requirements

Each plant with an asterisk by its name is a *seasonal* plant, meaning that the plant needs a dormant (or rest) period every year. At this time the plant should be put in a closet or a dark corner of the basement for six weeks to six months. Check with your local garden center as to the length of a particular plant's dormant period.

Light Requirement

Low—amount of daylight is not enough to read by
MEDIUM—readable daylight but no direct sun
HIGH—an east or north window area receiving two hours sun daily (or north window is unobstructed)
VERY HIGH—a window area receiving more than a half-day of direct sun

Water Requirement

DRY—soil becomes moderately dry between watering almost to bottom of container
MOIST/DRY—soil is evenly moist *but not wet;* then allow to dry about one-half the depth of container
MOIST—soil is quite moist and is never allowed to dry out